PRELUDE TO BRESSINGHAM

PRELUDE TO BRESSINGHAM

by

ALAN BLOOM

TERENCE DALTON LIMITED
LAVENHAM . SUFFOLK
1975

Published by
TERENCE DALTON LIMITED
ISBN 0 900963 60 3

Text Set in 11 pt Baskerville Typeface

Printed in Great Britain at
The Lavenham Press limited
Lavenham   Suffolk

Contents

Index of Illustrations

To the memory of my parents who taught me how to enjoy work.

Chapter One

THE village roads were not tarred in 1914. They were dusty in summer, and if some people went out to see a motor car go by, all kept their doors shut to keep out the dust. The roadman swept it into little heaps and barrowed it on to larger ones, and for a few coppers my father sometimes had these carted to use as potting soil, since cow turds and horse droppings were included in the sweepings. It was the same with winter mud, except that the roadmen used scrapers and shovels, and when that dried out it was just as good for potting if not better, because tumbril carts dropped both muck and mud as they passed. Sometimes, the roadmen would scrape it into a ridge to one side of the road because it was too soupy to shovel until it drained out a bit. Such a ridge, freshly scraped, was lying alongside the road as I came home from school one day, and met old Ingle Dash. He worked for my father as odd job man, including shoe cleaning for the family. Because he grumbled once again about the mud on my boots, the devil took me and I made them dirtier still by walking in the roadman's ridge of muck. "I'll tell yer father, I will you, young dav'el", he growled. He did and thereafter I had to clean my own shoes first thing after tea.

It was not until well after the 1914-18 War that the roads were tarred to put an end to both dust and mud. We lived in the High Street of Over in West Cambridgeshire on the edge of the Fens, and when this or any council road needed making up, granites were used. These came by rail to Swavesey Station and Prime Godfrey with his fussy, clattering steam engine hauled trailers to wherever road-making was in progress. He would unhook a full trailer and take an empty one back, so that with three of the iron-wheeled vehicles and a dozen or so men loading and unloading a shuttle service was maintained. Men then spread the granites three or four inches thick, with others bringing in sub-soil with horses and carts. They scattered soil over the granites and it was then up to the traffic—nearly all iron-wheeled and hooved, to bed it down. This, my father explained, was the Macadam method of road making, named after the Scotsman who invented it on the principle that with at least one flat surface to a piece of broken stone this was bound to settle that side up, even if it took a year to achieve it.

Soil, and what lay beneath the surface including water, fascinated me. But as a seven year old boy, it was mainly speculation within the confines of my little world. I was not to know how much of my life would be spent in moving soil, and digging holes and trenches to find water, or dykes to be rid of water — to dig sometimes for the joy of it; at others in desperation, quite apart from using soils of many kinds in which to grow things. Now that I've had close on sixty years in intimate terms with earth in many forms, from mud to dust, clay, chalk, sand, gravel and rock, I'm no less fascinated by it. Much of the toil and sweat I could look back on as a waste of energy, because it has brought so little reward other than experience, and this may not count for much now that machines can do almost any job of earth moving. The change from the manual to the mechanical has been so complete that unless someone like me puts the former on record, the latter has no background.

Water, the geologists have said, came first; then mud, followed by soil or earth. As a small child, the first patch of open water I saw was one of the village ponds. There were several, handily placed where winter rains would fill them up and where cows on their way to and from pasture could drink along with the great slow gaited horses farmers used. A ploughman, sitting astride one of a team of three horses would let them drink before and after work, which might be half a mile away or more. The horses went right in, and the man just sat there waiting while they sucked up water made muddy by their hooves. The water was muddy all day, because it never had time to settle before cows or a passing cart splashed into it, apart from the ducks that swam about for hours on end. It was a thrill for me, when with my father in his high cart, I was driven into the pond.

In a very wet time ponds spilled over on to the road to find a way down to some Fen ditch. But in droughty summers they dried up, and those who had no well were in trouble. The first dry summer I remember was 1911 and that was the first time I saw a pond dried up. It was at a four cross roads at a corner of the Green, and with only mud to be seen, it was obvious that after all, the water had not been any deeper over the far side, as I'd been warned it was. The surface had a brownish grey film over it which was beginning to crack, revealing a jet-black mud beneath. When told it was going to be dug out I extracted a promise to be shown how. When the time came, I saw men with shovels throwing it up like lumps of black jelly into tumbril carts. Carts were backed in, and as one was led away another was ready to keep the men going. It was to be tipped on to the fields belonging to farmers who had lent horses and carts, and when dry, my father said, it would be spread to improve the land. They were taking two or three feet of mud out, down to the hard clay bottom, and it wouldn't need doing again for another twenty years. It was in fact dug out again at the end of the even drier summer of 1921, and being fourteen, I could sit on the high rear bank and watch the men at work for as long as I wished. It was then that I learned that the pond had other uses, for now and then a man would fetch out something that had been thrown in on dark nights, such indestructible articles as old kettles, women's stays and a rotting bag or two with a brick and a skeleton inside of a cat.

The ponds most often used were the ones to be dug out in dry summers, but there was one that never dried up and was never dug out. It had a bad name and even when it froze hard, no boys dare go on to its ice. It lay beside one of the roads to the Fens, and was very deep, they said where some pussy willows hung over the far bank. In summer it was covered with a film of duck weed, though no ducks ever fed on it. But at any time, it was said, children who went too near were liable to be pulled under by a hobgoblin who lived in an invisible lair, who shot out a long rod with a hook at the end. Once hooked the child would be dragged under and drowned. It had happened before, a long time ago, and could happen again.

My two brothers and I were warned about certain muddy ditches. One of these ran beside a meadow nearly opposite our house. It was a field we often played in, but having been warned against falling into the ditch, one naturally became inquisitive. The word diphtheria meant very little at that time. Even if some children had died of it, we never knew them. The ditch had steep sides and was not very wide and having peered into it, we decided that it stank too much ever to risk falling into it. A long stick revealed that there were only a few inches of murky water and below that was black, slimy mud a foot or so deep. There was a hedge on the far side, and once when birdsnesting I jumped across expecting to hold on to a stump near the nest I'd spotted. But the stump was rotten, and I fell back to find myself on hands and knees in the bottom of the ditch, with the thing called diphtheria adding to the fear that rose with the stink as I imagined what my parents would say, or do. There was more, much more said about diphtheria as my mother tried to get the rest of the mud from me, after father had scraped off the worst outdoors. I was put to bed, not knowing whether as a precaution or a punishment or both, and if I was out and about next day, it was a week before fear of diphtheria and death left me. A few years later two out of three brothers who lived close by another of those foul ditches died of diphtheria. And when at their funeral service we sang the hymn, "There's a friend for little children. Above the bright blue sky," there was a lump in my throat.

Long before that, I'd seen open graves in the churchyard. Except for one period of a few years when I had a real terror of death, graves were of interest, because they showed how the earth changed, from soil to subsoil. I thought too, how clever it was to be able to dig so deep and so narrow a hole, in so perfect a rectangle. The top soil on one side, and the stoney clay which began about half way down was thrown on the other. The Church School I attended was right opposite the church, and with a funeral most weeks of the year, there was sometimes the chance of seeing the gravedigger at work, much preferring to be there when the grave was being dug than when it was being filled in. I too wanted to dig a deep hole, just for fun, but my father wasn't keen to let me. Over the next thirty years or so, I dug many a hole of various kinds and for various reasons, and yet, when I was offered the job of gravedigger in Canada, I turned it down in spite of being desperately hard up.

The village name of Over meant a bank or shore, and it lay on a low promontory, sticking out with flat fenny lands on three sides. Most of the upland was of clay, known locally as gault. To the west, a mile away was the Great Ouse River, and as I was allowed more to roam, I came to know, not only the varying types of surface soil, but what lay beneath as well. There was a gravel pit just before one reached Bare Fen. This was an area of several hundred acres which had been enclosed in the seventeenth century into little grazing fields with high hedges. It was of special interest to me, for the fields were still of pasture, good for birdsnesting, and in some there were sweet smelling purple orchids and other wild flowers growing in spring and summer, and mushrooms in autumn.

It took a long time to get on sufficiently friendly terms with the graveldiggers. The shortcut footpath to Bare Fen passed quite near them, but at last I was allowed to pause and watch them at work, provided I did not get in their way. They spoke little between themselves and it seemed that each man stuck to his own job and got on with it at a steady, but almost relentless pace. Eventually I learned that they were on piece work, and it was on the heaps of screened sand and gravel that their wages depended. The field was slowly being eaten into by these men, half was already on a lower level by six feet, from which four feet of gravel had already been dug. There were two planks sloping down from the higher, undug part, to the lower, and with a barrow each a man wheeled up a load of freshly dug gravel which two other men were digging from below with shovels, which they first had to loosen with forks. At the top was a screen propped up at an angle of about 45 degrees and on to this, each barrow load was thrown, a shovel full at a time. The browny orange stones rolled back and the sand trickled through the screen to make two heaps which had to be separated by boards as they grew higher and the screen raised, till the heap was judged large enough. Mostly the men took back an empty barrow down the second plank so as not to fall foul of the other man coming up loaded.

When the rectangular section they were working on was down to water, they would begin another section. The method then was to take off the top spit of soil and run this out on additional planks to a previous section, which had been dug out, but on which the second and third spits of subsoil had already been tipped. It was all very systematic, for having placed the top soil where it would again make pasture, the subsoil, down to where the gravel began at two or three feet deep, would be placed in a section that was worked out, so that it again became subsoil, but at a much lower level. With each section about five yards by three or four, the whole field was gradually being lowered in level, section by section, and above were neat heaps of graded sand and gravel, ready for sale. It was sold by the cubic yard and when customers came with horses and carts, or the owner delivered with his own, there was seldom any argument as to what level the tumbril should be filled to make a yard load, since all the tumbrils were locally made to the same size and pattern. And if it was a labour to load, the carts could be 'umpundled' by slipping out a wooden rod which tipped up the load on to wherever it was needed. Every few years loads were tipped on the paths bordering the village streets, and when spread this too had to be bedded down by people's feet.

Almost on the crest of the low clay hill to the south east of the village, there were brick pits. It was a place wild with brambles and bushes, with hillocks and hollows, the lowest of which held water, with newts and moorhens. It must have been there a long time, for many of the buildings in the village were built with the grey-buff bricks it still produced. It was run by two elderly men, and one of them, Mo Hard, was a man boys had to avoid. They lived alone together in a cottage near the road, and left it together once a week on a Saturday afternoon, so we knew when it was safe to roam there. The clay they had dug and shaped by hand would be mostly standing as unbaked bricks to dry—or to save up until they had enough to close up the kiln and fire them, which was only about twice a year. Once the bricks were shaped, barrows were used for transport, but to bring the freshly dug clay to the open shed with its bench, a narrow railway track and trucks were used which had to be pushed by hand, and which we played with some Saturday afternoons.

Near the brick field stood a windmill. It was owned by a Mr Mustill who also owned one in Swavesey a mile away. He was a kindly man, and when we saw the sails of his Over mill turning, we could be sure he would at least let us stand and watch him at work, cleverly hoisting up sacks of grain to the top, and seeing how it emerged as flour from the spout below. Close by, the St Ives— Cambridge railway went through quite a deep cutting, and from the road bridge above a good view of passing trains was another attraction to that part of the village. There was still a great heap of clay, which the railway navvies dug from the cutting, lying on top. During the First World War, word went round that this was to be burnt to make it into rubble, though what purpose this would serve was never properly explained. We were allowed to see the great open fire that was made and when well alight to watch men dig and throw lumps of clay thickly on top till only a small hole in the middle remained for smoke to escape. This went on for several days, but ended without explanation, and without using a hundredth part of that great bank of blue-grey gault, thick with bushes where once I came across at least a score of snakes, in a writhing heap. Why so many should squirm together was not explained either.

Only two fields away from the gravel pit, was one belonging to my father. His bent was in horticulture, and though he kept a general village store, his heart was in growing fruit and flowers, and this was one of two fields where both were grown. It had been pasture and in one corner was a small pond almost trodden in by generations of cattle. At about eleven years old I reckoned I was man enough to dig out at least part of that little pond. It held no water in summer, which was when his crops most needed it. This time he agreed, saying it would be very handy when planting during a dry time if I could make a deeper hole and find water. I hoped to find gravel too, because it was much more interesting material than clay to dig. There was the chance of finding a fossil, though I'd never found more than a piece of an ammonite in Johnson's gravel pit.

For three days I dug. The first day after breaking up for summer holidays, was spent in throwing out clayey mud lumps made hard by the compression of many hooves. I began with the intention of digging out at least half the pond, but by the second day had decided to cut down the area to a quarter. Still clay, with just traces of gravel, but though I'd only dug down to about three feet, on the morning of the third day, there was a little water in the bottom, which had seeped in overnight. Reducing the size of the hole again I dug feverishly, as more water appeared with more gravel. I took off my socks and working with boots soaked I left off that evening with a hole only three or four feet across, but with two feet of water I reckoned there would be next morning, I was happy. It was my first real hole and it would be a real boon, even if water for planting was not the sole reason for digging it.

Water was a vital factor in the minds of almost everyone in Over. There was no piped supply, and all but the few households which possessed a well had to use one of the village pumps. The one we had to use was shared by close on a hundred out of the nine hundred inhabitants of the village. One used it for drinking, but for washing one had to rely if possible on rain water storage butts. The nearest pump to our house had a handle of iron that swelled out to a large heavy pear shaped end. The idea was that the weight would ease the pull on the downward stroke, but it was too heavy and too high for small boys to lift. This made me think that any gain its weighted end achieved on the downward stroke was cancelled out by the extra effort it took to raise it again. The well from which the water was drawn was a hundred and fifty yards away in a field, and the pump often produced no water. You could hear it clanging a long way off, and by its tone knew whether or not water was coming out. Even when it did, and when I was old enough to use it, it was very hard to get a drink from it. The spout was high up, pointing downwards and by the time you got the handle down, what water you'd raised had left it and run away. The pump near the Church was better. It had a leaden spout, sticking out from a wooden casing, and in this was a tiny hole. All you had to do to take a drink was to hold one hand tightly over the spout end, make a few strokes with the handle and a jet of water came from the little hole over which one's mouth could close and drink. It was said that the well for this was close by the churchyard wall, but no one objected and treated the implications as something of a joke. On the score of pollution, the few households with wells of their own preferred to use them regardless of the fact that muck heaps or pigsties were within seeping distance. And the owners were frowned on if, on the well giving out in a droughty time, they too came to a parish pump with buckets.

A grazier and dairyman named also Mustill was often under suspicion when he used a parish pump. He kept three or four scraggy cows, but had no pasture of his own. During the day he followed them as they fed off grass verges anywhere in the village, keeping up with his three-wheeled push cart. When evening milking time came, he squatted on his three-legged stool and emptied the results directly into the ten gallon churn on his push cart, and having brought the cows home, added the morning's yield and began his round. His was the only milk round, but he didn't have many customers, because it was said he used the parish pump to make supplies go farther. Certainly, he showed signs of both poverty and disregard of hygiene, and I often saw him pick up a piece of dried cow turd to eke out his pipe tobacco. The Law eventually caught up with him. It put a stop to milk adulteration, and he ended up in the workhouse.

There was a larger dairy concern, and another parish pump stood just outside their farmyard gate. It was often my job to fetch the family milk when our house cow was dry, as well as take any surplus to this dairy when she was flush, since they purchased milk as well. I once casually asked father why, when they emptied milk into their own measuring bucket with its brass calibrations inside, this was always stood on a certain flat stone. He said he expected it was because it was dead level for correct measurement, but I had my doubts after a while because the bucket was invariably adjusted on the stone to face one way. The dairyman left me standing one day, having been called indoors by his wife, and with no one looking I turned it the opposite way and proved that the stone had a half inch slope, which gave the buyer maybe half a pint more than he recorded for payment. Father was furious about that, and went with me next time with a spirit level, which told no lies, and this put a stop to their artful dodge.

It was during the summer of 1921 that the village really felt the pinch, for only one rain fell between Easter and Michaelmas, and that did no more than lay the dust. In that spring, father had a well of his own dug in the yard, to act as storage for roof water, even if it yielded none from below. The man who dug it said it wouldn't and he was right. At two feet down he came to bluish-grey clay, and this meant, he said, that however deep one went, there would be no water-bearing gravel beneath. At about twelve feet, it was bricked round and covered over, with a drain pipe to lead in the water from nearby roofs, but it was not until after the drought of that long summer, that enough water ran into it to be of use.

The well on our Willingham road field was dried up before mid-summer. This had been dug when father planted the four acres with fruit a few years before, and it was on heavy clay land where only certain flowers would grow between the tree rows. The ten foot deep well was useful so long as there was soak water to draw from, for spring planting and for the few pigs father kept there, as well as for a greenhouse in which he grew tomatoes and chrysanthemums in turn. But in 1921, with wells and ponds dry and village pumps prohibited except for drinking water, it became a daily task to dip water from the one main ditch on the edge of the Fen which still had some. During school holidays, I went with Billy Webster who worked for us, down to the Chain ditch with our two-wheeled trolley, with barrels and tanks. It was a mile from the Willingham Road field and it took two of us an hour to fill up, since the one who dipped the bucket had to hand it up to whoever tipped it into the tubs. It took more than two hours one day, when, having almost filled up, Tom the horse decided to back away from a wasp that was worrying him. The cart and tubs just missed Billy standing down beside the steep banked ditch, and I jumped clear of the trolley as it went over the edge of the culvert, leaving Tom almost suspended by the shafts and harness. As we freed him, another horse and cart came for water, and with this help, we were ready for filling up once more, this time with a lump of willow wood behind the wheel, for a prop.

Tom fell into the well not long after that. Having brought up a load of water to the Willingham road field, he was unyoked while the day's consignment of plums was made ready to go to Swavesey station in 28 lb. 'half-sieves' of wicker. Tom had his nose bag and was hitched to a post, but broke loose without being noticed. The nearby well was covered only with boards, and they were no match for his hind legs, even if he was only fourteen hands. Down he went. Hearing a noise we rushed out to find him squatting on his haunches at the bottom of the ten foot well, with his forelegs wedged to the side, level with his head. A rope was suggested, but it would only go round his neck, and if the three of us could have pulled Tom out it would have choked him. "Poor old Tom," father said, when someone came along and said he'd have to be knackered where he was and then hauled out. As a family, we were fond of Tom, who was well over twenty years old, and had a character of his own. "If he can be got out dead, he can be got out alive," said father and sent me down to Wayman's the builders' yard, asking for the loan of shear legs. Hours later, with the three poles and pulley and ropes above Tom, after throwing down little clots to make him move his front legs so that a rope could be got behind his shoulders, up he came with me helping to haul on the pulley rope. Father sent a report of the accident to the *Daily Mail* and we were all disappointed that it was never published.

With summers over, summers in which the threat of water shortages were like a spectre to father because there was nothing he could do about it, these were often followed by winters when floods were a menace. The Great Ouse had its source a hundred miles away, taking water from five counties. At St Ives four miles distant as the crow flies, the Ouse Valley opened out into a flood plain which, broadening still more at Over, became the Fen country. Until the seventeenth century, no concerted effort to drain the Fens had been made, but under Charles I, the 'Gentlemen Adventurers' banded together and employed the Dutchman Cornelius Vermuyden as chief engineer. The Adventurers were to receive seventy-five thousand acres of the land to be drained, and having surveyed these southern Fens, Vermuyden began the work in Over and Swavesey Parishes, by raising banks. One high bank led at right angles from the river to the edge of the promontory on which the village was built, so as to dam up flood water and hold it back as a reservoir. Several thousand acres of grazing land could be flooded up to four or five feet deep, for as long as it took the river to cope with the excess, rather than allow it to rush into and across the wider Fens, which were to be drained. This area became known as the Bedford Level, named after the Earl who was one of the chief investors, and across it a new bypass river twenty-one miles long was dug and embanked, to re-enter the Ouse at Denver where a tidal sluice was built to prevent conflict between land water and sea. In and around Over there remain houses, built for the drainers, of unmistakeable Dutch or Flemish design. And I took pride in the family tradition that my Huguenot or Dutch ancestors were said to have come over with Vermuyden to drain the Fens and stayed there.

The work was not finished until Cromwell's time. It could even be said that it took three hundred years to finish, for part of Vermuyden's grand scheme was to divert the tributary rivers that joined the Ouse in the peaty fens and during flood time make them empty into the tidal part of the river further north beyond Denver Sluice. Maybe the Adventurers wished to claim their land with no more outlay, but whatever the reason for this part of Vermuyden's scheme not being carried out, it was the shrinkage of the peat fens through drainage that caused endless troubles until it was finally finished in the 1960's.

It was a mile from Over village to Overcote Ferry, though this is a ferry no more. The *Pike and Eel Inn* on the Huntingdonshire bank was said to have belonged in the old days to Cromwell's Secretary, and until 1930 it was no more than a riverside pub, nestling amongst silver-leaved willows. This was by far the shortest route to St Ives, even if one had to wait for the ferry, paying tuppence for the ferry boat crossing, or sixpence with horse and cart using the drawbridge. This was pushed across by men's feet. The fixed chain, from bank to bank, passed through a set of rollers at each end of the drawbridge, and with a deft flick, one could wrap a disc at the end of a short chain, on to the heavier drawbridge chain, and by pulling in the opposite direction from which you wished to go, the feet pushed the drawbridge over. It was a slow almost musical process, with the clicking of the chains, and the driver of the cart more often than not would pick up a spare pulling chain and help himself as well as the ferryman.

The slow moving Ouse, so prettily flanked by the tassel-headed Scirpus rush, and with its yellow water lilies, with a fascinating variety of other aquatic plants, to say nothing of fish, was the greatest of all temptations for me, as a boy, to shirk work and duty. My father was a keen angler, but he had a keen conscience as well, and I grew up with the same conflict within me — between sweet but unproductive pastimes and the rather dour necessities entailing work, that built up the latter as a virtue. But there were times when free of mind and light of heart, I could roam at will and let imagination run as new discoveries were made. At such times, I would not have changed situations with any other boy in England. I could see how fortunate I was to live in a village with so much to offer. With leanings towards anything to do with land and water, with history, geology and geography thrown in, every opportunity for discovering what that increasing freedom provided must be taken advantage of. These were of course phases and crazes that came as bonuses to basic interests, and one of the latter was to feel a pride in being a member of a community which has fought for its land.

Chapter Two

THE people of Over had been fighting for centuries for their land, and when word went round that the floods were out, I wanted to be with the men who watched over the flood banks. Webb's Hole was the name of one of the two sluices that helped to contain the floods. It had heavy wooden gates which could be opened to let the river water spill on to those thousands of acres of grazing fens, in Over and Swavesey parishes. When the river level began to fall, then the gates would open of their own accord, but for weeks sometimes, there would still be water on those pastures. On some there were lesser sluices, called fobs. These were single doors wound up or down, and for Mare Fen, to the south of Vermuyden's big bank, the water was mostly held back in hopes of skating. The sixty acres of Mare Fen was one of the famous places for the Fenmen to hold their skating matches. For speed they had been champions for generations, and with Swavesey station so near and handy, skaters came in their thousands.

Overlooking Mare Fen was an abrupt corner of upland known as Mill Pits, a place of holes and hillocks, the origin of which was held as a mystery. The tale that it was from there that Oliver Cromwell's cannon knocked the top of Swavesey church tower had to be discounted when the Vicar pronounced that it never had a spire. If the mystery remained, Mill Pits served as still another place to play in with imagination adding zest to exploration.

The watercourse which ran past Mare Fen was called a Catchwater Dyke. It ran at the foot of the uplands and to the side of the Fen against which it was embanked. This was an obvious diversion, similar, but on a much smaller scale than Vermuyden's idea of keeping control of flood water before it reached the lowest parts. It followed the contour of the upland slope for a mile or two, and since it took the water from a large area of these low clay uplands, was itself a means of filling the wide flood reservoir, which sometimes left the embanked railway track to St Ives a mere ribbon across miles of water.

It was in this big dyke that I first saw Germans. They were prisoners still dressed in grey uniforms and wearing their little round forage caps, and it came as a surprise after all we'd been told about the Germans, that but for their dress they could be taken for ordinary men, who could laugh and chatter like anyone else, even if they were under guard as they dug out the mud and barrowed it away. From there over the low hill on which the village was built, in line with the hundred and sixty-five foot spire of Over church, the Fens widened out. The road to Overcote Ferry went over the hump made by the Barrier bank, and in flood times, this was where people came to see the sight, with the swirling river water eight feet higher than the land which the bank protected. It was a quarter of a mile from bank to bank, though on the Huntingdonshire side the land itself was a little higher. A mile downstream was the last sluice before Denver twenty miles to the north. Over people called it their Staunch but on the map it was Browns Hill Staunch, nearer to the Huntingdonshire village of Bluntisham than to Over. Bluntismere, or Bluntisham Fen, had its own pumping engine — as had Over Fen. Both were driven by steam, and their chimneys belched smoke day and night during flood time.

The Staunch played its part in controlling the river and the lock keeper could only break his isolation by boat during a time of high flood, and even with his house being built on an artificial mound, the water sometimes came into downstairs rooms. The pumping engines drained each parish fen. They were placed at the foot of the Barrier Bank so that excess water in the Fen, with its system of main and secondary dykes, could be lifted into the river, through a kind of trap door in the bank, as a big paddle wheel revolved. The Over engine, at the extreme north of the parish, opposite from Earith village, was placed there in 1838. It was fascinating to watch the rhythmic piston pushing up and down the massive beam above, which transferred the power to a crank. This in turn revolved the great paddle wheel, encased outside the building, and it was only this that made a noise as each wooden paddle hit the water and scooped it up. The engine worked so smoothly and silently with its moving parts gleaming brightly in the dim light and with its smell of smoky steam and hot oil, it was a place to linger in for as long as one dared or was allowed to. Such privileges depended on the man on duty, and sometimes it only took an offer to break down big lumps of coal ready to shovel into the boiler furnace to gain it and at the same time to enhance the proud feeling of belonging, of having a part to play in the fight.

Not far from the pumping engine was Earith Suspension Bridge, and the Hermitage Sluice. This was the point at which the Bedford Rivers, Old and New began. The Old Bedford was cut in Charles I's reign, but when work was resumed after the Civil War, Vermuyden found it to be inadequate and with the help of Scots prisoners and Dutchmen, dug the New Bedford, a little way to the East. Between the two lay the washes, and with each river having an outer Barrier Bank, the intervening strip could also be used for penning up excessive floods. The Hermitage Sluice was built to prevent the Ouse from following its old meandering course. It was almost twice the length of the cut direct to Denver, twenty-one miles to the north, skirting the Isle of Ely, which stood out on clear spring days as the green island in the midst of black fens. Willingham, the next village to the east of Over, had its pumping engine on the banks of the old river and all the way to where it joined the Cam, south of Ely, these engine houses stood every few miles, to keep their parish fens safe for crops and stock.

It was in Willingham Fen that Hereward the Wake was said to have fought a battle with the Normans. Belsars Hill was there and when the Normans tried to get to Aldreth Causeway and on to the Isle to subdue the last Anglo-Saxon stronghold, Hereward and his men thwarted them by subtle skill, causing many a foe to drown. Tales and traditions led to conflict in my mind. At times I was torn, as urges to be a drainer and a cultivator of land fell out with leanings towards those fenmen of old who were a race apart. The men who lived in and from the wild, swampy fens as they were before the drainers came, conjured up romantic fancies in my mind. They too had fought, though they had lost, and had of necessity become cultivators themselves, they had a cause and part of me vainly wished it to keep alive.

But such fancies changed. The sight of a gang of men digging a new dyke, or deepening an old one, could do this. There was such skill in the way they worked, for even if the dyke held water as well as mud, they could make a job of it by means of 'stanks'. These were dams of clay or earth, perhaps with planks to help. The men set out a day's work by placing a stank some distance ahead, and with one left behind the previous day, they would empty the length between with buckets. Thrown over the stank behind, water could not run in from either end, and with only mud to contend with work began. Special spades cut out chunks of mud—or clay if that was the subsoil, and with a flick of the wrist, without raising the spade very high the chunk would fly up well over the bank. There were usually four men in a gang, but more if because of extra width or depth a stage called for extra men to throw beyond the reach of these below. Such men knew how to catch a lump on their own shovel, as it came up from the digger on the bottom level. Much of Over Fen had no 'staple' — no basic subsoil, for a great depth. It was a mixture of flood — clay and the peat of decayed rushes, speckled with fresh water snail shells. To collect these and to look for what else might be dug out was another excuse to linger and often hunger sent me home when the men left off to eat their meal of half a loaf, with a raw onion, lump of cheese or some fat pork, as they squatted beside their plaited 'docky baskets', backs to the wind. To some of the men with whom I liked to linger or chat as they worked, no doubt I was a nuisance. To me some were dour and surly, and if I offered to help, there would be a curt refusal and I'd be told to hop it.

A fascination for steam engines often prompted me to enter a farmyard where one was at work with its threshing tackle, and an offer to kill off mice and rats as they ran from the stack might lead to being allowed to squat in the coal bunker of the engine for a rest. It all depended on the men in charge, and those who were tolerant and friendly generated a warmth in me so that I would do almost anything they asked of me. There was a shortage of men for landwork during the First World War, and farmers were glad to pay a shilling a day for boys of my age to load harvest carts, or muck out pigsties. I spent one Saturday forking out muck at an isolated farm a mile deep in the Fen. I'd not told my parents where I was going because I didn't know, and had just wandered off. The farmer's wife asked me to stop to dinner in payment for two hours work, and with the job to finish I stayed on to tea as well. But retribution came after dark, from parents whose anxiety had mounted to bring punishment both for working elsewhere when father could have done with my help, and for lack of thought for their fears. Not long after, and not far from home, a smallholder enticed me in to muck out his pigsties, telling me he'd pay me for the job. It took me three hours and having told me I'd made a fair job, gave me threepence, which made me decide it would be more worth while in future to ask father what jobs I could do.

As a side line, he grew mustard and cress in his greenhouse during the early part of the year. Preparing the beds for sowing was my first experience in handling soil as a gardener. The bed had to be dug over evenly and patted down, and when the seed was scattered, a thin sifting of fine soil covered it. Such soil was not easy to find, and with road scrapings and sweepings too rich, and in any case needed for chrysanthemums or tomatoes, it had to be dug from a hole in the garden between two yew trees where even in winter it was dry enough for sifting. By May, with the cress season ended, soil would be barrowed back from the greenhouse to fill up the hole where it stayed until after Christmas to be dug out once more. It was through having to sell the little bags of mustard and cress from door to door on Saturdays, that I came to know more about the village, its people and what they did and how they lived, as well as what lay behind some of the high fences and walls, which many yards and premises had, flanking the village streets. So much was going on, so many different kinds of work, from the women of the house, to cobblers, carpenters, blacksmiths, wheelwrights, harness makers, thatchers, roadmen, to say nothing of those who worked on the land, and in the orchards for which the district was famous. With so much work in evidence, and with work regarded as a great virtue, the few sluggards were more despised than whores and drunkards. I wanted to earn a reputation too, as a hard worker like my father. And as I grew bigger and stronger, there was pride to be taken in my capacity for work and endurance, rather than for sport and games. This came at some cost to scholastic progress, and it shaped my attitude to school as a place of useless restriction, and I longed for the day when I could escape from authority, and have no more of that tedious daily journey by train to the Cambridge school I attended. I wanted to be a man, working for a living, for working I believed, was living.

I played truant more than once, unbeknown to my parents. One spring day I went to the same fen farm where I'd spent a whole Saturday forking muck, and joined in with three men hoeing thistles from a field of winter wheat. Another time, I slipped into a gateway on my way to the station and instead of going to school I stayed well screened from the road helping as a strawberry picker. The last time was to help the ferryman to mend and tar a boat beside the river on a hot summer's day, and two weeks later, before end of term just before going up into the fifth form, I left, with only a wink of connivance from father as permission, saying it was a waste of time to stay at school when he needed my help.

Working for father was not after all very enjoyable. It was July 1922, and I was close on sixteen, and came in for leading Tom pulling the cultivator between rows of fruit trees and market flowers. I came back just right too for plum picking, and for cutting, bunching and packing for market such flowers as asters, statice and early chrysanthemums. Prices had slumped and day after day came back sale returns that scarcely covered the cost of packing and carriage. It was my job to take the fruit and flowers to Swavesey station, where in a siding twenty or thirty box wagons were being loaded by other growers, mainly of fruit. Good Czar and Victoria plums were making only ½d per pound, and though all agreed it was mainly due to glut, none would agree to stop sending for a time to ease the situation and give prices a chance to harden. Instead, more and more were consigned until in the end some gave up, but by then the people in the big towns were fed up with plums and would buy no more.

The year before, with only half a crop, prices had been good. That was the year of the great drought, when ponds were dug out, when horses and carts could ford the river instead of using the draw-bridge, and when water was so scarce. It was the year in which Tom fell in the well, and the well in the yard at home had been dug in vain. I'd had no hand in this, but I enjoyed digging a trench in the orchard behind our garden. It was time, father said, for the privy to be emptied, and if I liked I could dig the trench. Our man Billy Webster had found a mate to help him one night on extra pay, plus drink and all the cigarettes they wished to smoke. It took several evenings to dig that trench, three feet deep, ten yards long and three feet wide.

The privy was not far away—though well away—from the house, as such privies mostly were. It was densely covered with ivy, and the little room had a low bench in which were three holes, graded in size for adults and children to sit over. As a small child it was a little terrifying when my imagination ran as I peered into those dark smelly holes, for they were deep. Later, by the light of the candle we used on dark nights it was creepy, but by setting light to a piece of paper and dropping it into a hole, one could see that it was not so deep after all. And by 1921, with a family of six, plus a maid, plus other day-time work people using it, it was obvious the time had come for the pit to be brought back to its original depth.

Billy Webster didn't mind the job, he said, for he was not so long back from the war in France where such a job would have been pleasant compared with some he d had to do. Yet to me, as well as to my younger brother George, it was an exciting event, and on the night sleep was elusive, because I had visions of Billy and his mate finding it was only half finished by morning. But in the morning there was no sign of Billy, and behind, in the orchard, my trench was now a long mound of earth, like a grave. It was there, in the following year that father grew the finest celery he ever remembered which prompted him to remark once more how wasteful we were for not using human manure as did the Chinese.

By far the most noisome stink near home was that which came through the hedge bordering the little orchard. The next door property belonged to Wayman Brothers, who were builders by trade. They lived in identical new houses across the road, but their yard was flanked by cottages and fronted by a big old Flemish style house in which the Waymans had previously lived for centuries. This and the cottages were let. The latter had no back door and about twenty people shared one privy at the end of the yard. This narrowed in to a pathway, past various sheds used by the Waymans into their orchard. There had been a shallow ditch beside the path and into this, the emptyings from the communal privy were pitched till it spread into an ever larger and longer heap — with only a hedge between it and our little orchard and only fifty yards from the back door of our house. This, together with father's yearning to have done with the shop keeping he'd been forced to follow, and go in entirely for market gardening, made him decide, in 1922, to sell out and move.

It saddened me, to think we should be leaving Over with its river and fen. I'd already begun business in a small way on my own account the year before, by taking over the mustard and cress and early radishes. From the profit, I'd bought a gilt and she'd reared a litter which showed a little profit too, even if the eight week old weaners had to go at only eighteen shillings each, because pig prices were low at the time. When the second litter arrived, and the sow decided to eat them, I sold her for £10 and bought a new bike with the money, and it was on this that I cycled to Oakington during August 1922 to see the new property my parents had just bought. It was only five miles away, and having seen it decided that after all I would not miss Over so much, because at Oakington soil was light and friable, and underneath there was sand and gravel holding abundant water, and there was a well that never ran dry.

This visit seemed to crystallise my ambitions. After many a change of mind I decided on horticulture, fully believing that I had all the qualities needed to make a success of it. I reckoned that the fenman's attitude to work, thrift and business sense was an ideal worth nursing regardless of the type of business one was in. I couldn't see myself as being brash and priggish but others must have put that kind of label on me. With hindsight I know it was deserved and maybe this was one of the reasons why my parents thought it best for me to leave home to gain experience. I'd said that the market garden aspect of horticulture, whether fruit or flowers, did not appeal to me. Rewards were too chancy, for no matter how hard you worked and how good your production was, you were at the mercy of the market. Produce was sold on commission through agents in the big towns and cities, and one simply had no say in fixing a price. The agent and his customers had all the say; the grower had none at all. This was a very sore point with father too. He once made a valiant effort to start up a jam factory, but was beaten by bad luck and lack of capital and his mail order business for asparagus, plums and dried flowers proved too exacting and troublesome.

To grow hardy plants for direct sale, rather than flowers, was the thing for me — to be a proper nurseryman, fixing my own prices and not having to cut the flowers just as they were coming out. There was one such nurseryman in Wisbech and a week or two before my parents moved to Oakington, I went to work for G. W. Miller of Clarkson Nurseries. The wage for a fifty-six hour week was ten shillings, and with board and lodging at twice this amount, I was still a drain on father, and had to keep a tight hold on the pence. Through some mistake I first went to what was little better than a common lodging house, catering for casual labourers, mainly Irish. For a greenhorn it was rather terrifying to find there were four beds in one room, and though I was told to go into one double bed when I went up at 10 p.m., I woke later to find a drunken Irishman in with me, and the other beds all occupied too. I stayed only one night, for Harry Giles, the man at the nursery with whom I was put to work next morning, took pity on me.

Wisbech stands on silt land. This was brought in by sea floods soon after Roman times, and as each flood left its deposit the level was gradually raised and the penetration of muddy sea water gradually receded. Until the drainers got to work, the black peaty fens inland were as high if not higher than the silted up fringe to the Wash. But drainage of the peat brought about shrinkage too, and so little by little the rivers passing through the peat had to be embanked against flooding. The silt did not shrink but the rivers through this had still to find an outfall to the sea, which over the centuries continued to recede, making the fringe wider and the Black Fens behind more and more difficult to drain and cultivate. This silty area, now up to fifteen miles wide in places, is without doubt the most fertile in England, yielding prodigious crops. In the years after 1875 when straight farming showed a poor return, the silt land farmers went in for much greater variety in fruit, vegetables and flowers. Their land, they said, was too good for corn crops even if the yield was higher. G. W. Miller's nursery was of only a few acres, and included plums, apples, strawberries and raspberries as well as a variety of hardy plants grown for sale. These were grown in beds six feet wide and, as a novice, I was shown how to dig and plant on this short row system, which was standard practice in nurseries at that time. A vacant strip had to be set out with lines along each side. A shorter line was stretched across one end and after taking out a couple of barrow loads of soil from one end and tip up at the other, twenty yards back. Then with spades we began to dig up to the cross line and, having buried muck and weeds, the soil beneath the line was patted down. With a spade backed up to the line, a little trench was cut out, pulling the soil forwards, and in this the plants were inserted nine inches apart. Mr Miller himself—an old man with a snow white beard—had prepared the plants. They were heucheras, a few varieties of which father had bought from him, because of their cut flower possibilities, but those in the tray behind us had been cut into crowns to grow on for a year to sell as plants.

The silty soil was soft by comparison with anything I'd previously dug. There were no stones and it kept the spades we used shining bright. In Over a spade was almost impossible to work with. If the soil was moist it would stick to it, and if dry, it was so hard that only a fork would penetrate. Even the lighter Oakington soil would not keep a spade bright—which was it seemed, the crucial test of whether a spade or fork was the best tool to use. Here in Wisbech, not only did the soil cut cleanly with a spade, but it was possible to push it in deeply without having to use the foot for pressure. Harry Giles used his heel and told me to do the same. "You get more pressure and you won't wear a hole in the instep or sole," he said. But though I did as I was told it was slower. He had already chided me for going too quickly saying it was best to keep a steady pace, which was a lesson I've tried to learn over and over again since then.

As a bed progressed, working backwards, the flanking paths, two feet wide, had to be skimmed free of weeds and these were buried as we dug. The skimming and the digging left the bed just a few inches higher than the paths on either side, and this edge had to be patted so that it followed exactly the straight line of string with which the bed was marked out. Sticks, cut twelve inches long, acted as measurements between each row and as each row was planted, pressed in and smoothed over with freshly dug soil, so the cross line was set back, using the stick at each end for exactness of measurement. And if the next door bed also held plants, then each row in the new bed had to be perfectly in line with those across the path.

This batch of planting ended after a few days and I was put to weeding alone. It had been showery weather and not good for hoeing. Weeds grew with at least equal luxuriance as plants — annual nettles, fat hen, chickweed, groundsel and annual grass predominating. It was tedious work and, having several heaps of weeds along a path, I asked Harry Giles if I might dig a hole and bury them. He was an indulgent man and said that since Mr Miller and the Manager Jack Battersby were exhibiting at some distant Flower Show, I could and showed me a place not far away. This was my chance to see what was beneath this silt which the sea had brought in centuries ago. King John had lost his Treasure somewhere in the Wisbech area and I might just hit the very spot. I dug an oblong hole just big enough to stand in and keep digging and having begun decided to go as deep as I could before being stopped. It was such easy digging that in half an hour I was five feet or so down and apart from there being a yellowish tinge below two feet, the subsoil was no different in texture from the top.

I was probing deeper still in one corner of the hole when Harry's voice from above startled me as he said I'd get him into trouble if it got to Mr Miller what I'd been doing and I'd better look slippy and fill half of it back — and be sure none of that yellowy stuff was left lying on top. It was after I'd stuck to my weeding a few more days that Harry told me how in places this silt was fifteen feet or more deep. Wisbech, he said was more or less floating, because once down to where the subsoil silt was waterlogged, it was like quicksand. Workmen had been known to leave tools in the bottom of a trench overnight and next morning they were sunk out of sight. In places, peat could be found below the silt — very compressed by the weight above, but usually it lay below the water table. As for King John's Treasure, the chances, he reckoned, were ten million to one that it would ever be found, because this too would sink in the quicksands below. Harry Giles was a Cornishman but he learned a good deal about Wisbech since coming there to live. The town claimed the title of "Queen of the Fens" and "Capital of the Fens", but to me this seemed lacking in justification. I would have said Ely, because it was a Cathedral City, dominating splendidly on its own Isle, surrounded by the true black soiled fenland — a place of refuge in times of strife. Wisbech, flanking the river Nene, could well have been non-existent when Etheldreda came to found her Abbey at Ely in Saxon times.

Chapter Three

WISBECH was an interesting place for me, but that interest did not last. After three months, with the prospect of winter ahead with shorter days and less interesting work I yearned for home, and to begin to work up a stock of hardy perennials, to have more freedom. Father was willing enough, saying that there was a vast amount of work to be done to make the six acres of land at Oakington capable of producing a living. The property had cost £1,800 and there was very little to live on from the sale of his Over assets which came to not much more than this. Stocks of plants had to be moved before winter and two days a week he and I went the five miles with horse and trolley to dig them up and replant them at Oakington. The journey took nearly an hour each way, in spite of Tom being replaced with a younger horse. Father's worry over shortage of money was somewhat offset by his joy of at last being free of the shop. If he made a mistake during that first winter of spending too much time and money in making a garden around Meadow House, he could scarcely be blamed, but it did result in stringencies later on. Though past fifty, he could do double the work of Frank, who apart from me, was the only helper he could afford to pay. My pay was five shillings a week pocket money, with keep thrown in, and for a time I was happy, especially as I was allowed to dig a sandpit.

Meadow House, Oakington, a very square solid affair dated 1860, had more amenities than Victoria House in Over, the walls of which as did most houses there rose abruptly from the street. The latter had no indoor water supply, though it was lit by an acetylene gas plant which father had installed and which apart from being dangerous had a habit of running out at the most awkward times. Meadow House had to be lit by oil lamps but at least it had a bathroom and water was always available indoors so long as the tanks in the roof were kept supplied by the hand worked force-pump, which took forty minutes of hard work to fill each day. Father did not like the idea of the indoor W.C., attached to the bathroom. The proper place, he believed, was outside and one early expense was to make

(i)   Priory Farm and cottage, Burwell—a typical fenland farmstead.

(ii)   A piece of the 300 acre Adventurers Fen which the author tackled, 1940-43 to reclaim for food production.

(iii)   First steps in reclamation was to clear the old choked up dykes.

(iv)   A look down Harrison's Drove towards Upware in January 1940 gives another idea of the challenge undertaken.

(v)   A pile of bog oak covering two acres of the fen during reclamation.

(vi)   The King and Queen and other distinguished visitors came to Adventurers Fen in 1942 to see the work of reclamation. The Author is seen talking to Queen Elizabeth, now the Queen Mother, whilst they watch bog oak being dug out.

(vii) New dykes had to be dug through the black fen by hand. By the end of the war a Ruston Bucyrus dragline replaced hand labour.

(viii) One challenge leads to another and the home made claying machine was such an example.

(ix) The reed infested land was cleared of bushes and other obstacles and then ploughed. The reed roots and bog oak turned up by the plough are shown in this picture.

(x) The Author's faith in the whole project showed in the first crops in 1943 taken from the wilderness.

(xi) Brook House, Fordham, Cambridgeshire. The Author with his sons, Robert and Adrian

(xii)   First sight of Bressingham Hall, 1947.

ii)   Bressingham was the second major challenge. Acres such as this had to be reclaimed and brought into cultivation.

(xiv)   The Author enjoying some spade work at Bressingham in 1947.

(xv)   The Author's parents at Bressingham in 1947.

one, using rain water from the roof to save pumping up the tank placed above specially for this outside W.C. This caused some inconvenience as well as conflict because soft or rain water was so much better for washing, and with another larger tank to catch what fell on the other side of the house, supplies were unequally divided. If the washing water tank ran dry in summer, there was pump water to fall back on, but when the W.C. tank fell empty, it was a problem, because the privy was just outside the pantry window, and either we had to replenish the tank by taking buckets of water up a ladder or stop using it, till rain came again.

The six acres that went with the house was all that was left of what had been a farm until just after the war. The previous owner had died and the County Council bought all the land and the farm buildings and split it up amongst four or five would-be small farmers — mostly ex-service men. The buildings were close by, with the enclosing fence only thirty yards away. These buildings the tenants had to share, with the huge old thatched barn going to the man with the most land. In theory this "back to the land" drive which took place in 1919-20 was a good idea, but in practice it was already showing up its weaknesses by the time our family settled into Meadow House, which, with the six acres, had not been bought up by the Council. Those men, having borrowed money with which to buy stock and implements went in when prices were high, but already it was clear that another farming slump was round the corner, if not already here. Wages had dropped from forty-eight shillings a week in 1919 to thirty shillings late in 1922, and the price of corn, milk and other produce had tumbled even more. The six acres had been set with potatoes by the previous owner and father had bought the crop at valuation during August. There was a bumper crop, but all he could get for them was £2 per ton, and part of the long heap which we'd picked so laboriously was left to rot for lack of a buyer.

The summer of 1923 brought a rebellion on my part against parental authority. The work of market gardening went against the grain, and with prices pitifully low, I could not see that it was up to me for the time being to make the best of a bad job instead of wanting as father sometimes said, to run before I could walk. I missed the river at Over, where it had been so easy to cycle down for a swim after a hot day or to go fishing on a Saturday evening. Sometimes I went, but the effort of cycling six miles took away much of the pleasure. There was quite a large ditch at the bottom of the holding, but having its source at Dry Drayton, it held very little water in summer. During a hot spell, I enticed one or two others of my age to help in making a dam so as to hold back the water behind, deep enough to swim in. But all we had after several hours labour was two feet which stirred up the mud so much that it was not fit even for paddling.

With discontent seething it began to dawn on me that to be a proper nurseryman further outside experience might be helpful, and late in 1923 I found myself crocking pots and weeding on Wallaces Nursery at Tunbridge Wells. An uncle living there had got me the job and some lodgings. It was a much larger nursery than Millers at Wisbech, and apart from the alpines department where I began, there were a few acres of herbaceous plants as well, though shrubs covered the largest area.

Where flower pots were used, a new boy's job was nearly always to clean them and then place pieces of broken crock over the hole in the bottom ready for men to use for potting. For preparing and mixing soil a boy was not trusted, but acted as helper to an experienced man. Soil for potting was brought in by horse and cart and stacked, if turfy, for a year. Leaf mould came from Ashdown Forest and sand from Reigate or Leighton Buzzard. All was measured by the bushel to obtain the correct amounts, with bone meal as fertiliser, to be turned two or three times by hand to achieve a compost. Such techniques did not strike me as labour consuming, because there was no quicker way at that time. Soil was not sterilised, and the resultant weeds which sprang up in the young potted plants also made for long tedious work. The frame yard contained probably a hundred thousand plants in small pots covered at night during winter with two hundred six feet by four feet lights, which another boy and I had to take off every morning and replace before leaving work. This task I loathed and though I liked handling soil, I put in for a transfer from the alpine to the herbaceous department as well as a rise from 15s. to 17s. 6d. a week. On the open nursery I worked, as I'd done in Wisbech, planting up long narrow beds, as helper to an experienced man. The soil cut cleanly with a spade, though it was heavier than the Wisbech silt. This hilly country, I learned, had a sandstone base and the thought of digging a hole to reach stone plagued me, and again I begged to be allowed to give way to the urge. Again cautious permission was given and between some large rhododendrons, I went down to four feet to find only yellowish shale and sand.

Tired of being a boy, and with a thrustful nature, I applied for another job in the spring of 1924, and was quite surprised to be put in charge of a small stock of alpines and to be propagator at Charltons Nursery along the Eridge road. This carried a 30s. a week wage, and though only seventeen I had no doubt I was worth it, if not more, until I made some rather glaring mistakes in my ignorance, which John Charlton was tolerant enough to overlook. The nursery here was a long narrow strip at the foot of the L.B.S.C. Railway from Tunbridge Wells to Edenbridge. Trains were frequent and somehow friendly, and I lodged with a man whose job was to tap wheels with a hammer for cracks and faults in the metal. At weekends I'd walk or cycle around, but most Saturday afternoons were spent with my uncle who had a large house and seven acres of trees and garden. At times I must have been a nuisance to him rather than a help, and I see now it is likely that he allowed me to make a rockery because my repeated requests wore down his resistance.

Much as I liked propagating and handling plants with care and patience, I was impatient to get on, to do things in a big way when such urges came over me, as they often did. The idea of becoming a landscape gardener appealed very much, but for this too training was necessary, and the thought of being under supervision and authority was not to my liking at all. On one of my wanderings, I came across a stream and seeing some lumps of rock in the bank, I enjoyed myself greatly making a dam until caught by the owner of the land, out for a walk with dog and gun. For the next half hour I had to place each piece of rock from the dam, exactly where the owner told me, and was then let off with a warning. On an outlying part of the Benhall estate I found a dam which had been there so long that what had been a small lake above it, was now growing bushes and sedge. It did not look very swampy, but in trying to cross it, I slipped from sedge tussock and went down into soft mud up to my waist.

With a growing longing to go north, I was accepted in a post offered at Malton, Yorkshire early in 1925, but only stayed there six weeks. The wages were £2, but I'd given my age as 19. The foreman, with whom I lodged, challenged my age one day, and I feared the worst. Brazenly I offered to show him my birth certificate (which I did not possess anyway), but he said not to bother, because he guessed I was twenty-one if I was a day, and why did I want to keep my age down, at my age? From Malton I went to R. V. Roger's

Nursery at Pickering a few miles further north—for less money because there was a much greater opportunity to learn about plants as well as to explore some entrancing moors just beyond. The nursery was on limestone, and though in the year I stayed there, I did very little digging, and a great deal of plant propagation, the experience one way and another helped to narrow the gap between my ideas and ambitions—and my age. I was just turned twenty when I decided to join father again at Oakington where he was still struggling to make a living from growing market crops of fruit and flowers.

It took seven years, from 1926 to 1933, to change completely from market growing to being a nurseryman proper—growing plants, and not the flowers they produced, for sale. It was one thing to set about working up stocks of plants to sell, but quite another to find buyers for them. When growing for market you could at least send to whichever salesman you chose, in the big town of your choice, even if returns were so often uneconomically low. But for plants, grown in a very rural village, there was no retail sale locally, and after persuading father, soon after my return home, to get a van on hire purchase, I attended markets in towns within a twenty mile radius whenever there was enough to sell—indoor pot plants, bedding and rock plants as well as some flowers. I spent my twenty-first birthday on Cambridge market, and the takings were 22s. for the day, after paying 5s. stall rent. The General Strike of that year and resulting depression was not conducive to working up a business, and my ambitions were slow to materialise.

Times were hard and work had to come first to make any progress at all. The village itself was poor because nearly everyone was dependent on farming, and this was in the depths. Wages were 30s. weekly for 52 hours, and men were being stood off by local employers who could neither afford to keep going in the old way of having lots of men and horses for farming, nor go in for more modern equipment. Signs of poverty were evident enough, but it was accepted as inevitable with little complaint on the part of the sufferers and even less concern from those who were in better circumstances. By comparison with farmers and small-holders we were at least on an increasing scale of business, and by 1929 had four or five helpers, even if the net profit on which to live was under £200 for that year.

My mother was thrifty and had been saving up, and when a nine acre meadow next door came up for sale, she bought it for £500—a good price but it was good land. Father was a firm believer in trenching, and decided that by degrees this nine acres would be brought into cultivation by hand. Three of us spent three winters on the work and it was not half finished. The method was to skim off the turf and with a trench begun in a low place, bury the turf and turn over two spits deep on to it. Whether or not he counted the cost in labour I do not know, but this way it must have cost more per acre than it did to buy in the first place, even if it was ready to plant as soon as dug. During the third winter's digging we realised that some quicker method was needed and a ploughman with a pair of horses was hired for the next season's intake.

The soil of most of this field was a brownish loam and held scarcely any stones—unlike the original six acres adjoining with sand and gravel beneath. The reason for the difference appeared in the hole I dug just after it became ours. A belt of greensand ran down from near Dry Drayton and this was the end of it. At three feet down the brown took on a gingery hue, and deeper still I found small pieces of ironstone and then water, above blue clay.

It was hard going to build up a nursery business, gradually increasing stocks in variety and quantity as more orders came from advertising in a trade journal. I had no doubts on either the quality of the Oakington soil or fears of losses by drought. Another well had been dug in 1922 by a professional to serve the two glass houses father had moved from Over. Water came in so fast at ten feet down through the gravel, that a hand pump could not keep it down for the man to dig more deeply. When four years later I began the first plunge beds of potted alpine plants, watering was accomplished by fixing a hose to the same semi-rotary pump above the wall. I had to get our helper to pump as I held the end of the hose squeezed in to produce a spray. It was not until 1934 that, with several more beds of alpines, a more efficient method had to be found.

By then, I had the place on my own and was married. Father, with an unselfishness I never gave him credit for at the time, decided to move again. True, he liked glasshouse crops best, but to take on a derelict glasshouse nursery at Mildenhall when fifty-nine must have taken courage as well. My younger brother George joined him there. He too had decided on horticulture, and with Oakington on my own, for which I agreed to pay rent until I could afford to buy, I saw the future bright.

Some progress was made, and in three years, I had not only forsaken market growing completely, but had gone in for plant growing on a purely wholesale basis with a catalogue containing over a thousand different kinds of plants. Ambitions were always a step or two ahead of progress, and yet there were times when I looked round for some extra project involving soil and physical labour. The first of these was to dig another well, complete with water tower and an engine for pumping. Till now, hand pumping had been a chore that seemed inescapable because of the capital outlay other power would involve.

The site for the new well had to be central for the beds of alpines, and no one could dispute my decision to dig it on my own. As I dug, the top soil was barrowed away for potting, the subsoil used to fill up one of the last of many sandpits I'd dug when sand and gravel was needed, but from four feet down for the rest of the way, it was sand and gravel, some of which would be used to make a concrete pad for the iron-work water tower to be erected nearby. The method of well digging in water-bearing gravel was to use a spokeless cartwheel in the bottom. On this was placed a row of bricks, so arranged that with each one offset by half an inch, the corner of one brick pushed into the side of another all the way round. When the row was complete as a circle, no thrust from behind would dislodge them. I had to make sure that this first row needed nothing but whole bricks to make the circle and after that in spite of bending or overlapping, by using the same number of bricks for each row, the walls of the well must become evenly perpendicular, and no cement would be necessary until the domed top was made.

It was hard but exciting work, and once into water at about twelve feet it was a case of working in thigh boots, scooping out gravel from the bottom with a bucket, which, dripping water, was hoisted up on a rope by a helper on top. As the bottom deepened, inch by inch the cartwheel with its weight of bricks sank too, but the water coming in from all sides brought with it sand and gravel from behind the bricks, and the danger of caving in increased the deeper I delved. The portable pump on top was no match for the inrush of water and before I was satisfied that it was deep enough I had to give in. From then on it was just a matter of adding circles of bricks standing on a plank which had to be raised with each course, till finally, I found myself on top once more.

The water tower, made of angle iron, was bought second hand, and this had to be assembled on the ground and somehow pulled up into the vertical position. It was twenty-eight feet high and with the five hundred gallon tank fixed we used the only method we could think of to erect it—by means of a snatch block on a pole, pulled by the cable of a steam traction engine. This proved to be a very tricky business, not only to obtain the correct angle and fulcrum between the top of the pole and the engine, but to ensure the feet of the tower did not slip when pulling began, and that it did not pull too far and topple over in the opposite direction. The concrete pad had been made ready with bolts set in to fix the feet of the tower and though the latter teetered frighteningly as it came up to the vertical, luck was with us and the thing was safely held. That tower became a favourite climb for me, to scramble up when I felt like it, and to look down over my little domain.

This was a much more vital and satisfying project than some I'd had previously—and since. It seemed I was prone to thinking up some scheme or notion whenever more ordinary work called for no great mental effort, leading my mind astray at the mere suggestion of monotony. Once the germ of an idea began it had to be followed as far as it could, though many notions never developed far through lack of funds or practicability. The rock garden I decided I must made in 1927 was some outlet for me, in the creative sense, but after a year or two, I saw it as a mistake. It was not really necessary for the business—it was troublesome to maintain, and after all layout of rocks, however natural looking the formation, were rather out of place in this flat, rockless countryside.

Then there was what my mother dubbed "The Boggery", which I made the year after. This was a small pond on the far side of the new meadow she had bought. It had originally been dug out for cattle to drink from, with the expectation that the boundary ditch would keep up a sufficient level of water. But cattle, over the years, had trodden down the banks and the bottom was dry in summer, though boggy in winter. I made little channels down to water, diverting the flow of the ditch, whilst digging up spaces between in which to grow moisture loving plants. It was tough work, but hopeful of success I planted it up, only to find that weeds, especially docks and thistles, grew far better than my choice selection of plants, many of which died in the first year. The fault I discovered too late lay in two basic factors, which this project helped to teach me. One was that moisture-loving plants need that moisture only during the March-October growing period, and here it was the other way round. The second lesson was that for good growth, soil needs to be open, so that roots can go down for moisture. Cattle hooves had spoiled the soil structure here, and in spite of careful digging, the lumpy, sticky stuff I'd moved had not become aerated, and broken down into fine particles which alone encouraged root penetration and good growth. So, though I'd done the work mainly in my own spare time, it proved to be a waste of time, except for some experience gained.

*　　*　　*

Some success in business allowed scope for one or two more ideas which though not of direct concern to the business, were fairly easy to justify on that score, even if this was not the real reason. The new field was all taken in by 1934, and nursery plants had spread over practically the whole fifteen acres. Though generally flat, in keeping with the whole parish, this field was uneven in level. At some time part of it had been ploughed into 'lands'. The origin of these undulations in level was often discussed as a relic of times when stretches of about twelve yards wide were ploughed once or twice to the middle, so that this was a foot or so higher. The hollow so caused was probably for drainage, but some said it was to increase the surface area. To me, this seemed unlikely because if a giant roller were to flatten the whole, the outward spread would be so slight as to make little difference and the soil in the hollows would be shallow and perhaps soggy, whilst in a dry time, the ridges would suffer most. As a farming practice it had already died out, and though other local meadows were still in this formation all arable fields at any rate had been levelled off by ploughing them back again. This is what I did, when the rest of this field, after hand trenching, came under the plough. Nearer the road these 'lands' petered out, but there were one or two low places and corresponding banks, and though only a couple of feet or so different in level, it was enough to cause soggy patches in wet weather. One low place had been dug level in 1928, and in it were found three Anglo-Saxon skeletons with a shield over the crushed skull of one. Oakington had been sacked by the Danes in 870, and experts believed this to be the scene of a minor battle or massacre.

Another hollow was larger and in 1935 I decided that this should become a pond into which drains could be led. It was about forty yards from what had been my Boggery garden. During a slack time, we dug it out into a hollow — about fifteen yards long and six yards wide, and using only hand trucks and barrows, dumped the spoil into the Boggery until it was levelled off. It took a fortnight's hard labour, and I'm pretty certain my helpers had uncomplimentary things to say about my determination to go through with the project. I was sure that sufficient water lay beneath that end of the field to keep up a level and having dug down about five feet found two feet of water slowly seeped in from the green sand subsoil, and below this was blue clay impervious to water. With the pond finished I began digging drainage trenches on my own. As I came to water, drainpipes were let in, and I began to feel some vindication. Not for nothing was our road known as "Water Lane", and having followed my eye for the direction from which to catch some of that underground water, I was convinced the productivity of the land so drained would be improved. In that year, at odd times, I dug about a hundred yards of trench, two and a half feet or more deep and when pipes were laid there was a steady trickle of water to the new pond, filling it to nearly two feet from the bank top, on which I planted a weeping willow and some waterside plants as well as aquatics, stocking it with fish caught from the Ouse at Over.

Other projects included building a brick soil-steriliser, but this was not a success for long. The soil became too sterile from the dry heat and too burnt, but the steam steriliser I bought made it too wet. I had still much to learn about soil and its growing properties under greatly varying conditions. We were using a great deal more soil for potting, now that stocks of potted alpine plants exceeded 100,000, but mixtures used were on a trial and error basis. At that time pots were known under numbers rather than by diameter. For alpines we used 60's, and sometimes 72's. This referred to the number of pots in a 'cast' when fired at the maker's kiln. 72's were almost the smallest pots made. They were two and a half inches across the mouth, whereas 60's were three inches, 54's were four inches and 48's five inches. Numbers went down with the size of the pot. At that time, we could buy 60's at 25s. per thousand delivered from Wattisfield in Suffolk by lorry.

It had by now proved cheaper to buy graded sand by lorry from Earith, seven miles away, than to dig our own and riddle it. Ours was not sufficiently sharp for horticulture anyway, and with a four foot overburden to move first it was obviously uneconomic when the right stuff cost only 4s. per yard or ton, delivered.

The next project was to install overhead irrigation for the nursery. I had tried my hand at channel irrigation in the dry spell which continued after the water tower had become operational. It was all very enjoyable to make little rivulets, digging here and embanking there to make water seep into parched earth, but it took up space and time and uneven levels were often frustrating and difficult to overcome. By 1936 I was able to snap up what was a bargain in 200 yards length of Kinnells portable irrigation pipe with holes for spray jets at intervals and this brought the need for yet another well, of larger capacity and sited at a more strategic point to cover as much as possible of the open ground nursery stock. A water diviner was called in, but the spot he indicated, with the recommendation to drive in a bore hole to about twenty feet, proved useless. The oil engine driven pump I installed ran dry in ten minutes and after repetitions of this, I decided to dig another well myself in a slight dip, thirty yards away. Tests had shown that the diviner had come to the edge of the gravel, where it merged with clay, but having at one time dug an earlier sandpit near my choice of a site, I went ahead and dug my new well six feet wide. The water came in at twelve feet and the sides began to cave in as I let another brick-laden cart wheel settle down. There was so much water that a Fowler ploughing engine had to come and with its big suction hose, suck out under steam whilst I dug down deeper and deeper. Caving sides became dangerous and I worked in almost a frenzy in the bottom with water rushing in from all around faster than the great engine standing above could cope with. The ladder was in my way, but it was the only escape route lest a big cave-in occurred, and when at last I gave in, as I came up the ladder two facts emerged. One was that I'd luckily chosen a good spot for water, which would adequately meet our need for irrigation. The other was that I'd taken a big risk in staying down there so long.

An interest in what lay beneath the surface had led me to buy a drift map of Cambridgeshire. It had puzzled me why so much water came in through the gravel at no great depth, when the map showed only a small isolated area of gravel subsoil hereabouts. From observations over the years, I decided that the drift map might be incorrect, and I fastened on to the belief that the River Cam, north of Cambridge, and the Old West River between Cottenham and Earith, were in fact linked underground by a seam of gravel. If this were so, it would account for such subterranean water even if, at Oakington, the seam was at its narrowest, about a quarter of a mile wide. I put the idea to a University expert, and having followed it up, he gave me quite a lift when he agreed that the drift map was faulty and my notion was correct.

By 1935 I was looking for more land. The nursery business was growing and this gave a further boost to ambition. When deciding to go in for hardy plants and alpines to the trade, it seemed only sound to stand by three basic principles. These were to produce a wide range of plants of the best possible quality and to offer them at a reasonable price with the promise of prompt despatch. It was clear now that, but for the threat of war looming up, there was a good chance of the business ranking as one of the foremost nurseries of its type in the country, but it could not reach that position without more land. The first addition was six acres vacated by one of the smallholders under the County Council. No other smallholder wanted it, so I became tenant. To this was added another five acres lying further back, of very poor and rather heavy land, which the owner was fed up with trying to crop. A bridge over the big ditch at the bottom of the nursery was needed for access to both fields and with this to build and new land to get into good heart, it kept my mind pretty well occupied for a time.

The first attempt to use this land for plants was however proof of its unsuitability. The soil was too heavy—too difficult to get into good condition for planting, and when lifted for despatch, plants carried too much soil on their roots which would not shake off, and this added to carriage charges. Practically all orders went by rail from Oakington station which was on the Cambridge—St Ives L.N.E.R. line, only a quarter of a mile away, and there were grumbles from those who had to lift boxes packed with plants—and from me when bills for carriage came. During the summer of 1936 I looked around for a fresh holding altogether. Suitable land for nursery work was very hard to find, especially with rumour of a new R.A.F. aerodrome taking over hundreds of acres to the west of the village. Thinking that a move towards the Midlands would be in the right direction, I viewed several small farms in the Bedford-Northamptonshire area, but all fell short of the ideal I had in mind that were within reach of the capital I could muster. Quite good land could be bought at £25-£40 per acre with house included in those counties, and though I discovered later that the right kind of land could have been had in Norfolk and Suffolk for much less than this, at that time I was averse to moving to the east because rail connections for despatching orders would have been slower.

The large fruit growing parish of Cottenham lay next to the north, three miles away; dozens of trolleys, lorries and carts came daily in summer to load fruit at Oakington station, but prosperity had waned even more by now for market growers. Some growers were grubbing up fruit trees, others were struggling, and a few were letting orchards look after themselves. One such orchard lay beside the road to Cottenham no more than a mile from my nursery. The owner was an elderly widow, and whereas I believed I'd struck a good bargain in obtaining this eight acres rent-free for a year, I realised before the year was up, her side of the bargain was by far the best. The proviso over the rent was that I would bear the cost of rooting up the old apples and pears and after that would pay £3 per acre per annum. What the total cost was of converting the land from a derelict orchard to an open field ready for planting I never added up. The trees were pulled out with the same engines which I'd hired for the well and the water tower, belonging to my friend Harold Papworth, but for weeks afterwards, several men were there cutting them up and burning brush stumps.

I fancied that, having grown nothing but fruit trees for forty years, the land once ploughed, would be fertile. It was not heavy and was in fact on another greensand area, with soil of a light brownish colour. One of the Cottenham men I employed remarked that this type of land was so hungry that if a ploughman dropped his jacket in the furrow and covered it up, it would be consumed by next morning. This came after I'd had the field ploughed and though some fertiliser was applied before four acres of phlox were planted that autumn, only a few had made the grade for sale quality a year later.

So it was that the search for ideal land had to go on. I began to explore the possibilities of fen land. My knowledge of the fens, other than the western parts, was scanty, and it now seemed likely that on the eastern side, there might be some akin in quality or texture to parts of Holland, where vast quantities of nursery stock was grown. Some of this I had imported, as stock nucleus, and noting the soil that came on their roots held particles of fine sand as well as black peaty stuff, I made a survey over the southeastern fens beyond the river Cam which flowed north from Cambridge to Ely.

It was in Lode Fen that I found soil very much like the sample bag of Dutch I carried, I also found a farmer who was willing to let me rent a field of six acres on trial, and by January 1937 nearly all of it was planted up with stocks of phlox, trollius, iris and other subjects I thought should respond to this rich looking soil, that was never likely to suffer from drought since it lay below river level. I had ideas of competing with the Dutchmen on very favourable terms, because this land was cheap compared with theirs and with plenty of men looking for jobs, there appeared nothing to prevent my building up a much larger business than earlier ambitions had encompassed. It had been quite costly to plant that field, since it meant taking men and planting material each day the eleven miles distance from Oakington, the last half mile of which had to be on foot because the fen drove was so soft and muddy. But I remained full of hope and confidence until March, when unusually heavy rains came on. The rivers rose and so did the north west wind which built up tides in the Wash so high that the outlet to the sea of inland water was reduced. The call went out for volunteers to sandbag the river banks, and I spent a night or two on the Old West River, scarcely daring to think what it was like in Lode Fen. The owner had discounted risk of flooding when I took the field over, but when I went to inspect I found all my plants under two feet of water. A bank had blown a mile away the night before and hundreds of acres were flooded. When the water finally was pumped out, the soil was panned down and thousands of young plants lay with roots exposed. All we could do, with the time available, was to trowel them in again, and fears that panning and loss of soil aeration would stunt growth proved later to be only too well founded.

This, I believed, was just bad luck, a coincidence that was not likely to recur. With the need for more land still gnawing and the conviction that such 'fenny' soils offered most scope for me with capital so scarce, I could not give in. There was no future for me in Oakington, except perhaps as a base, though the R.A.F. were still encroaching on the parish and Hitler was still encroaching over Europe, I kidded myself, as did most people, that war would be averted, there was some sense in the idea of taking a farm of a hundred acres or more — if war came to make food production take the place of nursery stock. Another search was made that summer, but it was not until autumn 1938 that I found a farm of the type I wanted, at a price I could reach.

Chapter Four

THE FARM which, but for certain misgivings took my fancy, was Priory Farm, in Burwell Fen, a few miles north of Lode Fen. It was on offer to clear up the estate of a large farmer deceased, and consisted of exactly two hundred acres. The price asked was £1,800, to include a foreman's cottage. It was, I later discovered, rather dear at the £1,600 I finally paid for it. For one thing the steading was with wooden iron-roofed buildings, situated over half a mile down a soft fen drove, which was deep in black mud in winter, but dusty and bumpy in summer. The breach in the bank which flooded my experimental field in Lode Fen had probably saved Burwell Fen from inundation, but much of this, too, was poorly drained. It carried a Drainage Rate of 32s. per acre which reckoned as capital charge on a twenty year basis at five per cent brought the cost of the land itself up by £16 per acre. Burwell, like so many fenland parishes had its own drainage system. There was an outfall pump and engine at the junction of Burwell Lode and the Cam at Upware, and the water level in these embanked rivers was up to twelve feet higher than the land.

This made the amount of lift from the dykes to the river a problem since the Burwell Commissioners' engine and pump were old and unreliable, and because so much of the land in their Fen had gone out of cultivation and was therefore yielding no Drainage Rate, they had no money either to deepen the main dykes or to install a more efficient pump. As an owner occupier of over fifty acres I was entitled to become a Commissioner and then learned just how precarious the position was for the future. Under the 1930 Drainage Act, a higher River Authority such as the then Great Ouse Drainage Board, was empowered to take over Internal Boards — such as Burwell Fen Commissioners — if the need arose. Within a few months of taking possession I saw this as the only remedy, though I made myself unpopular with some of the Commissioners by agitating for a take-over.

A third of the farm was marshy grass, and I purchased three horses, and a deep digger 'chill' plough. This began to turn over the driest fields in January 1939, until stopped by waterlogging from another threat of flood and burst banks. Ploughing was also hindered by bog oaks. These had lain submerged where they fell for about four thousand years when a rise in sea level broke inland and killed them. George Johnson, the ploughman, had to carry a pocketful of wooden dowels. If one of these was inserted where the trace chains hooked on to the plough, the dowel would snap and cause no damage to the implement. But some of these oaks had been mighty trees in their day, and had trunks up to three feet in diameter and in length up to sixty feet. They had to be dug around, sawn through, split and dragged away, before the field could be tilled and drilled.

The cottage was occupied by Sid King as foreman, at a 50s. a week, rent-free wage. At this time the basic farm rate was 36s. I thought Sid King was highly paid at first, but though he was a touchy man to deal with, the amount of work he accomplished in the long hours he put in, made me quickly change my opinion. For me, living twenty miles away by road, via Cambridge, such a man was a vital need, and though three other men from Wicken were engaged as helpers, it soon became obvious that my venture into farming would be touch and go as far as resources were concerned, even though the nursery at Oakington was still prospering. With hopes of peace even more a matter of wishful thinking that spring, we planted up a few acres of assorted perennials as a second trial. Those at Lode had scarcely been worth digging up, since so few had made any growth, but I saw no justification for not trying again now that I had land of my own to go at.

In spite of money shortage, of the poor drainage outlook, and the threat of war, I found a tremendous thrill in the realisation that I was now a farmer too. Sid King drove the old Case tractor which, when the arable land was firm enough to support its iron shod wheels, did most of the spring cultivation. As it became drier the soil was a delight to work. It had a soft silky feel and kept tools bright and shiny, even where there was no sand content — so different in texture to the tough and heavy fens near Over, or the upland clays which tended to cripple one's ankles to walk over the clods when dry and to accumulate on the feet when wet, till one had to scrape or kick it off. This land surely, would grow bumper crops, given a chance and I meant to give it every chance within my power. Though a novice at farming practice, I had a love for the land at heart and if this new venture was full of challenge, it was full of promise too. It had been sadly neglected but that would change as I learned to become its master.

Every field on the farm, except the grassland that ran up to the Burwell Lode bank, was surrounded by ditches. And almost every ditch was in need of restoration and deepening. I could afford to have only a fraction of the needful work done during that summer, and for this I took on Stewart Collins. He was a casual labourer as avid for piece work as he was for pint pots of beer. With his wife, two daughters and two sons, he lived in a single-storied shack of a house close by the back of Wicken Lode, which ran to join Burwell Lode to form the eight hundred acre block of land of which Priory Farm was a part. Towards the apex of the V formed by these rivers was nearly four hundred acres of the wild Adventurers Fen — the name referring to the seventeenth century drainage Adventurers. Most of this land had been dug for turf which for generations was a staple industry in this part of the Fens. When the land became too low from digging and when the demand for peat ceased in the 1920's, it was largely disowned so as not to incur Drainage Rates and was taken over by the National Trust as an adjunct to the famous Wicken Fen which lay just beyond the intervening Wicken Lode. The Trust did not wish for their land to be drained and much preferred it to remain wild with reeds, sedge and bushes. But since my land adjoined theirs to the west, along a boundary of half a mile, there was bound to be a conflict of interests.

Stewart Collins as a man, could be said to be a relic of the old fen-land—the type of man they called a "fen slodger"—rough of manner, coarse of speech, a prowler by nature with home-made rules of conduct. The whole family worked on the land, and with only two small bedrooms, it was a matter of amused conjecture locally as to how the six of them, all adults, shared. The living room was shared, not only by the family, but with hens and geese which also made a quagmire of the shabby approaches. But as a family, they were workers. Mrs Collins and her two daughters worked for me singling and hoeing sugar beet, but Stewart was an expert ditcher as well, and the first he dug for me was one which ran into a larger dyke called an 'enterline' which served as a feeder to the main 'engine' dyke or drain. When the engine at Upware was pumping, the water in the dykes would flow towards it, but within an hour of it ceasing to pump, the flow would be reversed as the levels built up again.

A non-return sluice was needed, I thought, to prevent water in the artery drains from coming back, but allowing it to flow out when the pump was working. I'm not much of a carpenter, but spent a couple of days rigging up a wooden flap attached to a float so that the flap would not only open to let water out of Stewart Collin's ditch, but would prevent it from coming back. But it was not a success, and I pressed the Commissioners again and again. Of the six or eight men at their meetings, only one allied himself with me in favour of drastic action being taken to improve the drainage of the whole of Burwell Fen, amounting to about three thousand acres, one third of which was derelict. When war was declared that September, the only bright spot for me in that most depressing autumn was the conviction that now the Commissioners' hands would be forced. It was clear now that this farm, without proper drainage, could never be productive, and in the knowledge that my nursery business was almost certain to be cut down to a fraction, the outlook was as grim as that winter which began to harden its icy grip as the year came to an end.

Normal work was at a standstill for weeks. Autumn orders for plants, even at cut prices, had been barely a quarter of normal expectations. Though by now, with thirty-six acres of plants and a catalogue containing 1,870 kinds grown and offered, I had achieved the target set seven years before, it could no longer count as any achievement. It held anything but satisfaction for me. I spent more time at Burwell than at Oakington from the time war was declared and during the worst of the winter, worked on ditching and clearing bushes from a piece of derelict land. I also tried to make sleepers for a narrow gauge railway as a means of better access to the farm, but found that bog oak, the only wood I didn't have to buy, responded to a circular saw by making the blade so hot that it buckled. This ruled out another project which had begun with more hope than practicality. Sometimes I went skating on the Lodes. Though not in the first rank of speed skaters, I could move fairly fast in my Norwegians and with miles of ice to skate on, sometimes alone, sometimes with others for whom speed skating brings a peculiar exhilaration, it was some relief from the anxieties of that period.

But as General Winter began to overstay his welcome came news that the Ouse Catchment Board were taking over Burwell Fen, and I knew then that with a little more patience the battle against water could be won. The old Burwell installation had broken down irreparably and this had left the Commissioners no option but to give in at last. Burwell Fen was intersected by its Lode, and the deeper it ran into the Fen, the greater the height of its retaining banks were above fen land. Its purpose was to collect water from the base of the low chalk hills on which the village stood and conduct it to the Cam, where a sluice regulated its discharge. There were three similar lodes to the south, one for the Swaffham, another for Reach, and the third for Bottisham, against which Lode a separate village grew up just above the fen, which went merely by the name Lode — where my experiences of these fens had begun in 1937. Swaffham Fen had already been taken over by the Catchment Board, and now that Burwell had given in too, the Board's plan was to link the two. The culvert under Burwell Lode, which brought drainage water from the southern part of its Fen to join the main drain to Upware, was to be deepened and have its flow reversed so that by means of another culvert placed under Swaffham Lode, all Burwell water would be drawn into the Swaffham system, and both the modern pumps it possessed would drain Burwell Fen efficiently.

Anyone in my position could see that if radical improvements were made to Burwell Fen drainage and if war came, there would be a call for every possible acre to be brought into cultivation. With over three hundred acres of derelict National Trust land adjoining mine, this too might well come in for reclamation. If that were the case, I wanted to take it on. It would take a year for the new drainage works to be effective, and it would take a year to bring Priory Farm into full production, but I let the 'War Ag' Committee know that if they took over Adventurers Fen, I hoped they would entrust the reclamation to me. The year 1940 was sad but momentous for many, but I found it difficult to feel for others, for in that year my marriage went on the rocks, and I was left sole custodian of my three children — all under five, with only paid help to look after them whilst I was absent at Burwell, as I was two or three days a week. And there was the increasing threat of invasion whilst the job of Head A.R.P. Warden for Oakington fell to me. Harvest that year was good. The dry sunny weather suited crops growing on low fenny lands, and much of the nursery at Oakington had switched to food crops already. The labour force had been reduced from thirty six to less than half that number, but it was still a going concern. It was sad to see acres of plants, so costly to produce, being ploughed under in favour of onions, lettuces and tomatoes, but one had to be realistic. After 1941 the demand for plants recovered surprisingly. But it was a demand that could not then be met to any worth while extent.

The spring of 1941 brought the offer I'd been hoping for. The War Agricultural Committee were to take over Adventurers Fen. I was offered fifteen per cent on reclamation costs as contractor and would become tenant of the Committee, paying rent as each derelict field became ready for cropping. I jumped at the offer, seeing as usual, the end of the task, the fields of crops, rather than the size of the effort it would take to bring this about. But being over enthusiastic, I turned down the fifteen per cent, saying that I would prefer to do the job at bare cost, hoping that a reasonable rent would be my reward.

It was exciting to watch the beginnings of a new main dyke being dug by a Ruston Bucyrus excavator. This was beside a grassy lane known as Harrison's Drove and it led more or less through the centre of Adventurers Fen. There had been a ditch along both sides, but as with those dividing what had once been fields on either side it was choked and overgrown, not touched by man for forty years or more. The dragline bucket bit deeply into the mass of sedge and reeds, fetching out first their roots, then the black, oozing peat and into shell marl or in some places blue buttery clay or 'bear's muck.' The latter was the fenman's name for the greenish brown strata lying just above the clay. It had a curious stink, and though its origin must have been linked with the first inundation that killed the oak trees, I never found out what went to make it. The shell marl was interesting. Fresh water shells abounded almost everywhere in the peat, but in places where pools had obviously held water during summer long ago, when waters receded elsewhere, fresh water snails had congregated and stayed there to die.

As water levels began to drop in Adventurers Fen, the obvious thing to do was to set fire to the reeds and sedge in order to get at the land below with the plough. They were tinder dry above ground one April day, and a steady east wind was blowing. A fire spectacle can cause excitement in many a human breast, and I was no exception — until it began sweeping across the Fen out of any control I could exercise. I knew it could not get over into Wicken Fen because of the intervening Lode, with its wide grassy banks, and I also knew no danger to human life or property existed. What I did not anticipate was the sudden reaction that came to my mind, as the fire swept across at a furious rate. Here was I, the man who as a boy, would have been aghast at such destruction of natural fen growth, at least at times when my sympathies were with the wild and untamed, romantic fenland. I realised that I still possessed a nature-loving side especially for birds and plants, and here I was in the act of destroying one of the very few remaining areas of fen as it was before the fens were drained. It was a sobering thought but there was no turning back now. I'd got to do my damnedest to make that destruction complete as quickly as humanly possible.

The fire revealed fully the extent of the old turf diggings. Before, trying to walk through the reeds and bushes was a tricky business, for the surface of most fields was ridged. The ridges themselves were safe enough to tread on, but in between were trenches hidden by decaying growth below which could be two feet of water. One of the older men who worked for me knew all about turf digging. He told tales of the hard, rough lives the old diggers lived cutting turf on piece work rates for the owner or lessee of these fields and we now had somehow to level off what they had left, as field after field was abandoned after about 1914.

Turf cutting was a summer time job. Land would be marked in strips about three feet wide, to be worked alternately. Having begun with a hole at one end the top ten to twelve inches was pared with a sharp, heart-shaped spade and thrown into the hole. Cutting could then begin, using first a sword-like knife, making a straight cut fourteen inches deep. And then with a becket, a spade-like tool with a wing so that two sides were cut at once, it resulted in a standard piece of turf fourteen inches by three inches by four inches, which had to be laid on the 'staddle'. This was the adjoining strip and had to be left to provide a place for freshly cut turf to lay and dry—a process that might take several weeks, each turf needing turning during that time according to weather. The staddle would come in for digging another season, but in the process, the general level of the land would be lowered. Some farmers sold their turf rights, and it was always stipulated how many turves depth should be taken. Depending on drainage conditions, it could be up to three, and some parts of Burwell Fen had been dropped by as much as five feet in level. This, of course, was the reason for its dereliction. The Commissioners had taken a mortgage in 1846 to install a steam pump for £12,000. The turf cutters had paid drainage rates along with the farmers, but these allowed only for interest on the mortgage and maintenance work. There was no indemnity to compensate for lowering the level by turf cutting and so it was that in 1939 there was still £11,000 owing on the original mortgage and nearly a thousand acres abandoned through turf cutting, now exempt from rates, because it was derelict.

Turf diggers' piece work rates varied from 1s. to 1s 6d. per thousand (six hundred to the thousand) and when dry, donkeys were often used to carry the turf to the nearest loading staithe on a Lode, to be taken to the many Fenland towns and villages served by waterways. The cutters mostly worked in gangs and often stayed on the job from Monday to Friday, living in an igloo type hut, built with grassy turves and thatched with reeds. Life was rough and tough, and it was said that a murder was committed years ago in Burwell Fen by one of these men, but neither body nor culprit was found. Sedge and reeds were also cut in the Fens — reeds for thatching and sedge for heating brick ovens. Fen litter was the term for summer growth cut as hay. This was mown by hand, and when dry it was stacked near a river bank to be cut into chaff and sent to feed London horses. But now after the fire, in place of the sere reeds and sedge in Burwell Fen, in which man beast or bird could be seen only from above, all was black and charred.

Back to realities and schemings to bring this three hundred acres into food production as quickly as possible, there was no time for musings. Fields which had at one time been farmed had to come first and leave the old turf diggings till last. With the excavator at work on a main dyke, I had to put field ditches out to piece work by some of the extra men I'd taken on, now that the water had somewhere to go. The method of 'stanking' out a day's work still had to be practiced, but the stuff they threw out in Burwell Fen was much lighter to handle than that at Over. Apart from reed roots, which were tough and deeply penetrating, one could push a spade into the black peat without the aid of one's foot. These men used specially adapted shovels. The corner of a new tool would be cut off so that the end was slightly rounded — to make what they called a frog-nose shovel. With knife-sharp cutting edge, reed roots were no problem, though the big sedge tussocks were a different matter. They called these 'hassocks', and with these a mass of fibrous roots was capable of growing to a great size and age. The clay bed of the Fen varied considerably in depth below surface. In some places the bottom of a ditch six feet deep and eight feet wide would be soft and black still with peat. Into this it would be possible here and there to push a rod down another four or five feet before touching the harder clay. In other places, the clay bed rose above the bottom of the ditch to within three feet of the surface.

Scarcely an acre of Adventurers Fen was free of bushes. In the reed beds and turf pits, sallows and buckthorn grew on the staddles, but on land which had formerly been under the plough, they were so thick in some parts that a short cut through them would take far longer than walking round. I asked a blacksmith to make a cleaver-like chopper so that by slashing at the roots, a bush would pull out easily. The men didn't take to this, and I had to admit that it was a rather heavy tool to use. We tried a snoose chain with a horse for the smaller bushes and a tractor for the larger ones, but so often the chain would slip upwards and come adrift. Finally the answer came with a hook with an edge which bit into the stem and did not slip, and the only snag with that was lack of power in the iron wheeled tractor, and it was not until a new Allis Chalmers 35 h.p. crawler tractor arrived that a satisfying clearance was made in a day's work.

It was all very exciting. Every phase of the work was fascinating for me, but my enthusiasm was not shared by everyone, either on the job or by family and friends who thought I'd bitten off more than I could chew. There were times when I wondered about that too, but kept it to myself. The War Agricultural was helpful in lending me a Prairie Buster plough. It was a single furrow deep digger with a long breast to give plenty of clearance for the stuff it had to turn in. Ploughing was preceded by an Australian contrap-tion called a 'Stump Jumper' consisting of a diagonally set row of revolving discs, which in turn bit through the surface but with each disc on a spring caused no damage if it hit a stump — or bog oak. The more land we ploughed, the more of these oaks we found. A tractor driver having felt one marked the spot with a stick and the two small gangs of men whose job it became dug all round it, in the hope that the crawler tractor could pull it out without first having to saw or split it. Bog oaks had been well to the fore in my boyhood fancies of the real Fens, the old Fens, but little did I think I would have so much to do with them. They were lying in all directions, some with roots still attached, others having snapped off to fall, leaving a stump in the clay. If, as was often the case, the men found water before reaching under the trunk, it made tunnelling under it more difficult. But that tunnel had to be made so that by passing a chain, with hook and ring correctly, the trunk would roll out with the pull of the tractor whereas a straight dead pull would make the tractor bury itself rather than budge the trunk.

Tractors, on this soft spongy stuff, were often in trouble and, when on a low field, it was safer to have two at work so that one could pull the other out of it became stuck. The War Agricultural came to the rescue when bog oaks of such size and numbers were found that we could not cope. They sent two men who had been trained with explosives and week after week, the sound of exploding gelignite could be heard at intervals. The largest tree we found was traced to a hundred and twenty feet, but one monster had been eighty feet to the first branch. There was always some thrill in seeing these trunks roll out, always in hope that something interesting would be revealed. But very little was found, beyond boar's tusks, a bear's skull and many an antler. Disposal became a real problem. It had little value as firewood because it was so tough and expensive to cut. On sudden exposure after forty centuries, the air made the outer wood shiver and disintegrate slowly into powder, though the core was extremely hard when dry. With abut two acres in all piled up with trunks and stumps I was glad for an antique furniture manufacturer to come and take two lorry loads away, for which he gave me a couple of tobacco jars turned up from the wood, and these are the only tangible reminders I have of that period when as never before, I was up to the neck in work.

It took two years to reclaim Adventurers Fen, and by the summer of 1943 it was all under crops of one sort or another. Most of the clearing work was done in winter, because from May to October, the crops already growing had first call on time and labour. After some failures when trying to put a regular corn crop on newly reclaimed land, it became standard practice to sow a smother crop, such as mustard or buckwheat. Both were very effective in keeping down resurgent fen growth, but both were very difficult to harvest. Neither would go through a self binder to make into sheaves like wheat or barley, and the next best thing was one of the old-fashioned sail reapers. This cut through the stems and as the crop fell on to the tray behind, the sails swept it into a swath well to one side so that the implement did not run over what had already been cut. The autumn of 1942 was wet. Indeed, the whole season had been wet, making things very difficult. Buckwheat had been sown late on Rothschilds thirty acres. This was a dense thicket of bushes and had been left almost till last for clearance, and though the crop grew well enough, it was slow to ripen, and much of it lay flat on the ground. It had to be cut in order to plough the thirty acres again ready for potatoes, and when mid October came, it was clear that not even the sail reaper could deal with it.

So it was that sixteen of us, each with a scythe, set to and mowed it by hand. But that was not the end of the trouble it caused, for it would not dry out to be safe to cart and stack. We turned it and heaped it like hay, but the weather was all against us, and in desperation I decided to make a long narrow stack, in which 'chimneys' were left. These were made by drawing up in every five or six feet length a straw filled sack, so that heat and moisture could escape. But by spring much of it had turned mushy and was scarcely worth threshing.

This was one of the snags of fen farming, but in contrast so was blowing dust. With drainage, the peaty suface becomes light and in spring when preparing for sowing in dry weather, consolidation was almost impossible. During March and April, westerly gales were apt to blow up, and gather such force over the dead flat landscape, that dust began to rise. The sky turned dark and dust penetrated everywhere. It was like a dark brown fog, and when it was over, one would find ditches filled in with fine soil including fertiliser and freshly sown seed. Sugar beet was the most vulnerable crop, and there was nothing for it but to sow again. One field had to be sown a third time and ditches had to be dug out again.

The next year, 1943, made good the losses 1942 had brought — when I began to wish I'd not refused the offer to contract for the reclamation at fifteen per cent on costs. I'd turned it down, imagining it would be the patriotic thing to do and to hope for some relief on the rent to be paid as the land came ready for a regular crop. But with a warm dry summer in 1943 the future appeared much more rosy and it was on this note that I wrote *The Farm in the Fen* that autumn. It was also in a spirit of optimism that I decided to go in for claying, the efficacy of which was well-known and proof had come that it would apply to Burwell Fen as well.

A much deepened main drain had been dug in 1941 beside the drove leading to the farm. Clay from this was spread to a width of twenty yards or so and ploughed in. When the field came in for wheat in 1943, the clayed strip was separately threshed and the yield was sixteen coombs per acre against nine per acre for the rest of the field which had received no clay. Ideas of a machine to bore holes to bring up clay would not let me rest. The old method by hand labour was no longer economic and with so much land in need of claying, the need for a machine specially made for the job seemed to make sense. Having no engineering ability myself, enquiries led to Billy Avey, brother of two of my helpers, who was willing to have a go. I hired a small barn in Wicken as workshop, and bought equipment to fit it out.

At the end of a year's work, the machine was ready. It was a strange looking contraption as it emerged from the farm, and was drawn down the village street to the lane leading to the Fen. A ramshackle bridge over Wicken Lode nearly brought catastrophe when one wheel dropped through and the thing heeled perilously over. Stewart Collins gave it a sour look as it went past his shack and when finally it reached the appointed field I felt that a great moment had come. The field had been carefully searched for bog oaks in the belief that this was a much greater danger to it than any risk that it might not work. But to begin with it did not work, and it took another day for Billy to make adjustments to the power drive and the angle of the spade lugs which were to bring out the soil and clay and the big boring screw worm loosened and fitted. Next day all was set to go, the much deferred hope was at last to be realised. But the one mischance in a thousand occurred. As the machine whirred and clattered noisily, biting into the black soil casting it neatly on one side, there was a bang and it stopped dead as a chain broke and we found that the steel worm drive had broken too. Perhaps there was only one bog oak stump left in the whole of that field, but that was what we'd hit.

This was in the early winter of 1944, and I tried another method of claying, with a home made trenching implement. The first one was not worth repairing with risks of this happening again, but the second attempt also failed for quite another reason. By that time I'd been told that, three years after the war, now nearly at an end, the National Trust would be at liberty to take over Adventurers Fen again. The chances of them having me as a farming tenant were very remote, and it was only too plain that it would be allowed to revert to the wild, for that was their objective. At that time I could but feel sore at the prospects my future as a farmer held. From running five hundred and forty acres in Burwell Fen, and the thirty-six acres at Oakington with reasonable success, suddenly the picture was clouded over. I never wished to go back to live at Oakington having moved to Fordham within three miles of Burwell late in 1941. But now knowing that Adventurers Fen would sooner or later go derelict again, I lost heart in my own adjoining Priory Farm as well. Some solace came from a piece of land I'd bought at Fordham, which with an acre of garden at Brook House, enabled me to make a start in working up stocks of plants once more, from the remnants I'd managed to hang on to during the war. The pull which plants had for me was proving stronger than the belief I'd held that never again would I wish to restore the nursery business. As a business it scarcely existed by 1945, but as post war enquiries from customers increased, there came more incentive for me to increase plant stock to meet the demand, though I knew it would take a long time. The only answer to the problem staring me in the face day after day, seemed to lie in selling out at both Burwell and Oakington, once I'd found a farm where both farming and hardy plant growing could be practiced.

Chapter Five

IT WAS the diversity of soils as well as the setting that appealed to me so much at Bressingham. The solid twenty roomed typically Georgian house stood well back from the road in a ten acre meadow with some fine trees to set it off. The two hundred and twenty acres included some sloping gently down to the south, to the valley of the Upper Waveney River two miles west of Diss in Norfolk. This was good sound loamy land, neither heavy nor very light, but just above the valley bottom it was a sandy loam which I knew would be ideal for nursery work. On the floor of the valley, half a mile wide, it was black and mostly sandy fen. Some fields were marshy grass, others had been ploughed but poor drainage had ruined the crop. There were several acres of alder carrs in which poplars, sallows and birches grew as well as alders. And there were over thirty acres of fen, with reeds and bushes quite as wild as that I'd had to deal with in Adventurers Fen at Burwell.

My first visit to Bressingham was in February 1946. Ever since I decided to sell out and move from Cambridgeshire altogether, one adverse circumstance after another had cropped up. I expected that Priory Farm would make a good deal more than I paid for it, since it was so much improved and since land values had gone up anyway. But the auction date coincided too closely with the General Election of July 1945, and the view was generally held that the new post-war Government would again let farming down. There was not in fact a single genuine bid, and it took weeks to find a buyer — a Hungarian refugee with determination to make a bargain in his own favour and it went for £6 per acre plus another £8 an acre due as a betterment road charge for a new concrete strip the War Agricultural had built for better access. The sale of the land was followed by that of the stock and machinery, and until this money was available in December, I dare not look for another farm. To this was the added snag of having a compulsory purchase order placed on the Oakington property by the County Council for building, which froze more capital assets for nearly two years.

But having seen Bressingham Hall and having been told by the vendor that the river was due to be deepened by three feet to make good drainage possible I decided I must have it. Even the thought of reclaiming the derelict fenny land appealed in the knowledge that if I did restore it, it would remain mine. But having paid the deposit, I had to wait till Michaelmas — October 11th — for possession, and if suddenly my interests and activities had shrunk till that time came, I had plenty to occupy my mind, not least of which were domestic worries.

During the spring I dug a corner of one of the fen fields as a test plot for plants. The soil was black, containing fine sand, and a sub-soil of this same biscuit coloured sand two feet below surface. I had of course dug holes all over the place on my final survey before deciding to buy. In places the peat was six feet or more deep, but it needed only a rod to test this, thrust down till something harder was touched. In others there were sandbanks, running obliquely across fields and though only a foot or two higher than the rest, I saw dimly that one day these would present a problem. If drainage was improved, then these low sand ridges would retain their present level while the peaty places would shrink and settle thereby accentuating the difference. Pure peat would be pretty sterile, especially if saturated or very dry as I'd learned already to my cost, but so, I thought, could a soil that was probably over eighty per cent sand. This could be too dry at a time when, a very short distance away in the same field, the shrunken peaty places were too consolidated, lacking in aeration as a result of too much moisture.

But such problems would have to be met when they arose. I was so taken with the scope and the challenge this place seemed to offer that any snags I perceived were pushed aside, and I chafed to get to grips with the business of moving and improving what was after all a somewhat neglected property and to rebuild the nursery business. The old bogey of water shortage should not arise, I thought, because the river, small as it was at this point could be pumped, if need be. The owner said there was a borehole for the house supply, sited just outside the kitchen window, which had never failed. It was pumped into the roof tanks by a noisy indoor affair which ran by electricity, the latter coming from batteries kept charged with an oil engine in a nearby shed. The farm buildings were close to the house, but the only water used for livestock came from a small pond, which was foul with mud, at the end of the sloping yard. There was a larger pond in a meadow just above fen level and this too was a feature I had my eyes on for improvement in due course.

On the strength of the river being deepened, I arranged with a contractor to come in that autumn to deepen the field ditches, so that there would be no hold up of cultivations for lack of an outfall. But 1946 proved to be a very wet year and when autumn came, bringing the great day for moving and occupation, the land was wetter than it had been in February when I first looked over it. Even the upland was sticky, and the first loads of nursery plants had to go on a freshly ploughed meadow which I would have preferred not to plant until the turf had rotted. So began the pattern of adversity which set in from the first. I'd fondly hoped, that with affairs left behind in Cambridgeshire reaching settlement, once the move began, the way would be clear to forge ahead with my schemes.

But it was not working out that way at all. I went to inspect the River Board's dragline at work a mile or two downstream and this was disheartening for the excessive flow through wet weather had made dredging largely ineffective. From Diss upwards the river ran between high banks of soft running sand, making a bottleneck for the wider part of the valley higher up. The spoil thrown on to the bank served to add weight which reduced stability so that with water-borne silt coming down too, the increase in depth was negligible and anything but permanent. Instead of the river level being lowered by three feet, I doubted if it would be more than a few inches and the field ditches I was having deepened in anticipation would have scarcely any better outfall than before. With the onset of winter, there was in fact a danger that the excavator on the job could become marooned and with that in mind the contract was cancelled by mutal agreement.

I'd hoped that, having had the ditches deepened — amounting to well over a mile — I could still afford to clean up the horse pond. Its banks were trodden in and though it could serve as an irrigation reservoir in summer I had a weakness for water as an amenity — for fishing, skating and just as refreshment to the eyes and mind, with abundant aquatic growth. So it was that instead of working with cropping in mind, that dragline spent a week enlarging and deepening a pond which could scarcely offset the loss through the water-logged fields it was not able to remedy. By the time the driver had done what he could without getting bogged in the mud he'd slung out, the pond was nearly half an acre in area, and around it I planted willows and other trees, leaving the mud and sand to be cleared away when it dried out.

It was, to say the least, a frustrating winter for me. After one bitter spell of weather in December 1946 I fondly hoped there would be no more. It disproved the old saying about ice before Christmas that bore the weight of a man would not return in New Year to bear the weight of a duck. In mid-January it set in again, and until mid-March the ice grew to become nearly a foot thick and long before that even skating on it had lost its appeal.

In coming to Bressingham I'd been anxious on the score of enlisting adequate helpers. By the time winter arrived however, twenty or so had joined me. They had been dealing with arrivals of nursery stock from Oakington and Fordham, till the frost set in, and were then switched to trim neglected upland hedges and ditches and making good the total lack of suitable nursery buildings. I realised that, the longer the frost held, the greater the rush would be when spring came, with at least twenty acres at fifty thousand plants to the acre to establish, as well as tens of thousands of pot grown alpine plants.

Late in January I decided to go ahead with reclamation work I'd intended leaving till drier conditions came. There were twenty acres on which I'd set my sights for clearance and when an offer came of some German P.O.W.'s who were badly in need of work, I told the Camp Commandant to send them along. But because of frost and snow all they could do was to cut down the smaller bushes on that twenty acres. The only trouble was that, with a free daily dole of cigarettes, they worked with such a will that the job only lasted two weeks. But funds too were running low. I'd bought a circular saw bench and saw the chance of selling firewood—if I could also find the power needed to drive it. The sight of an old steam traction engine being towed along the road for scrapping fortified the yearning I'd always had to own one. There had been neither excuse nor use and till now the notion that steam would soon be superseded had never occurred, but having decided that one of these old timers would fill more than one need, within a week a 1912 Burrell, unused since an overhaul, was unloaded in the yard.

The later story of "Bella" was a sad one, and is told fully in *Steam Engines at Bressingham* (Faber 1970), but until the frost gave way, she earned her keep, even if there was a disappointing demand for firewood in spite of the fuel shortage of that grim winter. The frost ended with a gale that blew down forty-seven trees, most of which had to be cleared because of access needs. But heavy rain came too, and this with the melting snow on soil still impervious through frost brought real trouble for me. The barrier bank in Over Fen burst and caused the most harmful flood the southern Fens had experienced for more than a century, but I was too preoccupied with floods at Bressingham to do more than imagine the tribulations caused to others. The pitifully inadequate Waveney, with water from over twenty thousand acres to surge into our bottleneck valley, it spread right across its floor, up to three feet deep. A field of oats which my predecessor had left for me to clear up because having been cut, the wet autumn had spoiled the crop, was swept into an adjoining alder carr. This was the only benefit the flood bestowed, because any cropping in 1947 of the hundred acres or so I had of this low land would be almost impossible. The upland suffered too. It was squelchy underfoot and at a time when normally planting would be in full swing, most of us were digging drains to be able even to get on to the land.

Looking back after nearly fifty years as a cultivator and a nurseryman I could honestly say that this was the worst possible winter I could have chosen in which to move a nursery. I'd got to make the best of a bad job, but as if to go the whole hog, that spring and summer were also about as adverse weatherwise as they could be. Spring till mid-April was both wet and cold. Squally showers by day and frosts at night made for sticky, unpleasant and inefficient planting. My planters were new to the job anyway and some could not get the hang of making trowel holes so that roots of plants went vertically down. The results of many being set with roots folded or not deep enough showed up as dry weather set in. By late May they were suffering and in many cases dying, with drought affecting them far more because only a few weeks ago, the soil was saturated. What had appeared a year before as good workable loam, was now clotty and compressed. In one field I'd been obliged to plant soon after being ploughed from pasture because existing arable was too wet, losses were serious, and even irrigation did not seem to help. The latter failed anyway, because in pumping up from fen ditches the spray nozzles of the pipelines became blocked continually with weeds.

It was then that drastic action had to be taken. I decided to sink the borehole which I realised should have been done six months before, not waiting till a drought arrived. But now I had to wait six weeks for a permit to buy the steel tubing needed for the borehole. In the meantime, I tracked down the continuing losses of plants — especially delphiniums — to wireworm and this revealed another omission. Killer dust for wireworm was obtained, but after two weeks a test showed that it was not doing its work. The wireworm was as active where it had been applied as where none had been used. Frantic telephone calls brought a representative who said his firm had sent the wrong stuff, and though the correct deterrent was soon afterwards applied the worst of the damage had been done and twenty-five thousand of the most expensive plants we grew had died.

By then it was July, and later that month the well-boring firm was allowed, by permit, to begin. I dug a shallow well, five feet deep and in the centre of this his boring iron was driven in by means of a rope on a loose engine driven pulley-cum-winch. With about three twists of rope over the revolving winch, he raised or lowered the heavy boring tool, which was suspended from sheer legs — a tripod fifteen feet high. By pulling on the rope the boring tool came up and by letting go it thumped down inside the tube. The latter was driven in by the same means, changing the boring tool for a rammer. By pouring water down the hole the teeth of the tubular boring tool dug more easily into the subsoil, but what came up had to be poked out before it was let down again.

It was a slow process, and after passing through flinty sand as the top subsoil, it entered boulder clay at eight feet. This was hard, and it took three whole days to penetrate the seventy feet strata, till chalk appeared. Having encased the hole with tubing well into the chalk, the operator said there was no need to ram down any more — the chalk was hard enough without it. But it became quicker work because another tool like a huge chisel reduced the chalk, as water too was encountered, into a milky paste and after two more days, the water level in the tube began to rise perceptibly. With it rose my hopes. I'd had to chose the site, because the operator refused to do so. Knowing how chancy it was, he wasn't going to take the blame for a possible failure. But now with the depth a hundred and forty-five feet, he reckoned that with twenty four hours pumping, the water might rise to pretty near the surface, as the chalky solution, just like milk, was replaced by the force of clear water from the underground streams lying in the mass of chalk.

It is, of course, the water stored up in chalk or limestone that makes artesian wells possible, but there has to be an overlay of some impervious material such as clay. This has the effect of holding down the pressure where the chalk stratum slopes downwards, and in puncturing the overlay the water from the chalk rises to find its own rest level. At Bressingham that rest level proved to be only two feet below surface on that great day in late July when it came to the rescue of thousands of languishing plants. The six inch borehole pipe proved to be capable of supplying sixteen thousand gallons per hour and if we pumped that amount all during the day, the moment the pump stopped up came the water immediately to its rest level again.

It was a godsend, and for me came as the first real break in the run of bad luck which had dogged me for a year. The irrigation sprays lines were kept busy, but since these would not use half the water available, I made some run into the enlarged pond, and set about raising the banks so that it would fill with water two or three feet above fen level. From there I dug irrigation channels into the adjoining field. This too, had been grass but because of the wet autumn and winter we had been forced to plough and plant it, since the fibrous grass roots always prevent stickiness. In any case across this field ran a sand bank, and though easy to work, it dried out quickly in that droughty summer and my irrigation channels brought badly needed water to this late planted field. But for the waste of land and the extra time taken to make and maintain them, water channels at near surface level have some advantages which overhead spraying do not possess. The moisture percolates down and spreads to the roots of the crop, and the top tilth is not compressed as it sometimes is by overhead watering. I enjoyed myself greatly, for several days, but was at last forced to conclude that it was not the most economic method of irrigating.

JAD. 74

Chapter Six

THOUGH my theme differs from that of *The Bressingham Story* (1963) there is bound to be some overlapping at this stage. The year 1947 was chock full of anxieties of one kind and another and though I could see clearly enough that I'd brought most of them on myself for being over enthusiastic and even rash, there was still enough incentive to go ahead with some of my schemes. One of them was to clear up the twenty acres on which reclamation had begun, now that the fen had dried out. When it was safe to take her weight, "Bella" the traction engine was driven down, and for a month she pulled out stumps and bushes. I dug a hole for water and for fuel any old willow wood or alder wood to be had for the picking up was used. My helpers hooked up "Bella's" wire winch rope and with only a little throttle, she would give a cough and out came the bush or stump. Sallow willows have a habit of rooting down as branches loll over and often these would split off, or if they came up whole, there would be a huge black umbrella of soil hanging on to its shallow fibrous roots. Alders were very different. They were not large trees, but their roots went almost straight down, clasping soil so tightly that it took a lot of getting off. Quite often, their roots would penetrate underlying sand as well, and having pulled a tree over, there would be not only a gaping hole four or five feet deep, but a ton or more of soil and sand attached to the root, to be taken off, so that it fell back into the hole.

It was hot, but very enjoyable work for me as engine driver. It was none too pleasant for those at the end of the wire rope. I had to be careful when moving the engine and more than once the great iron wheels sank in making it necessary for the wire rope to be fixed to an anchor tree so that "Bella" could pull herself out. If it was hot for me, it was no less so for those burning up the brush. With the experiences I'd had at Burwell of fires burning insidiously into the peat, the ashes from the burning of one day had to be scattered and the place dug over without delay. I'd known instances of fire breaking out a week afterwards, especially on dry ditch banks and since it will burn down to subsoil or to water an established fire has to be dug around as a deep trench to stop further spreading. Acres of fenland have been lost by fire in this way, and here I was taking no risks.

Such tasks were absorbing, up to a point. But as the summer wore on, I could not rid myself of a deep uneasiness of mind. So much had gone awry with this venture and though I knew that stability in the financial sense could only come from the nursery business being a success, I had a reluctance to give it all the time, thought and energy needed to restore it to pre-war status and prosperity. A nurseryman's life is a very exacting one if it is to succeed, and somehow my experiences of farming and reclamation seemed only to add to the difficulty I had in applying myself more fully to horticulture. My foreman had come from Oakington but stayed only a few months because his wife disliked the locality. A search for someone to take his place was unsuccessful, for very few men had the specialised knowledge required, as well as the ability. And because I too still had domestic troubles with three young children needing far more attention than I alone could give them, maybe this was a greater cause than any for my unsettled state of mind.

Under a Separation Deed I was not free to marry again. From 1940 to late 1944 the responsibility for my three children would have been overwhelming but for the time I shared the Fordham house with my parents. The last in a long succession of housekeepers and nannies was Myrah who had a small daughter of her own, and I believed that this would be the long term solution. But Myrah felt her position to be invidious. Hopes that the move to Bressingham would alter this were not realised, and home security for the children and myself was at times unreliable. As I tried to find a way to a more settled home background, the thought of emigrating came like a maggot in my mind as 1947 came to an end. On the face of it it seemed crazy to even contemplate moving from Bressingham after little more than a year, and after having placed such high hopes in finding it a satisfying way of life. But the maggot fed and wriggled none the less as I reflected that Canada had always appealed to my imagination. I liked the idea of pioneering and there were so many restrictions and frustrations to contend with in England that I fancied a new beginning in a new country would solve my problems and give the children an equal chance to succeed.

The first enquiries I made were in response to an advertisement in the *Diss Express* which invited prospective emigrants to discuss prospects existing in British Columbia, which was the very Province that appealed most to me. The advertiser said that land was cheap to buy even if I wanted especially a property with access to natural water and some virgin land. He painted a very rosy picture indeed and the C.P.R. Emigration official I later saw in London was obviously keen for us to go. With booklets, maps and other literature to study, I made up my mind and went to consult both my Bank manager and solicitor. The former advised setting up a limited liability company, and the latter put this into effect by raising a loan on shares. A manager and an Attorney could keep Bressingham going, since it was unnecessary and inadvisable to sell out, in case I wished to return.

I kidded myself that a good manager would not be difficult to find and that he might well make a better success of the farm and nursery than I, in my unsettled, unhappy state of mind. I did not see it as escapism at the time, nor did I agree in the slightest with my father's remark, when I told him, that it was a foolhardy venture! He and my mother were now in retirement at Sheringham, and had fallen in love with Bressingham, believing it was the ideal place for me and the children. I'd believed that too, in 1946, but not now, and as the spring of 1948 came, Canada was becoming an obsession. Obstacles to going kept cropping up, but they served only to increase my determination.

Spruce trees that had blown down in the gale of March 1947 were sawn into slats with which to make packing cases for the best of my furniture. The Bank manager beat a new restriction on taking money out of the country by posting my application just before midnight on the deadline date. I made arrangements for remittances to be sent regularly to Canada and wrote out an exercise book full of advice and instructions on running the place, to help the manager, still to be appointed. Several candidates were interviewed during the summer but none so far had come up to scratch. Then my Attorney, who had connections with another nursery, said that, as he would be in closer contact with a possible manager than I, once I'd gone, he should be the man to make the final selection. This he did, and though I was not at all impressed when I met his choice a few weeks before sailing date, there was nothing I could do but hope I had misjudged.

Having booked months ahead cabins on the *Aquitania*, sailing from Southampton on 9th September, and having cleared up my affairs as best I could, there was no room for a change of mind, especially as the children were so excited about going. There was the threat of an injunction under the Deed of Separation to prevent my taking them out of the country, but there was no one, as I'd feared, waiting at the gangway to the *Aquitania* to present me with the necessary document. And as the old ship drew away into the dusk I had the first inkling that, after all, I might be running away from reality. It had been much harder than I'd expected to pull up my roots, and though forty-two was not too old to make a new beginning, I'd no idea where our final destination would be, where I could begin again to put down roots. It was as well, just then that I hadn't.

The crated furniture had gone by freighter but we had between us twenty-seven pieces of baggage. This took a long time to get through Customs at Halifax, Nova Scotia a week later. It took a long and very uncomfortable twenty-seven hours to travel over the uneven C.N.R. tracks to Montreal. But on the smoother C.P.R., after a good night's sleep, the depression I'd felt pretty acutely lifted as I woke to see the lakes and forests of Ontario. This was the Canada I'd imagined and read about in R. M. Ballantyne's and John Buchan's books of years ago, and this Trans-continental railway was the one on which I'd always longed to travel. The drab immensity of the Manitoba and Saskatchewan farm lands was not so uplifting, as day after day the long train hauled by its magnificent red loco-motive drove on. But when at last we could see the distant Rockies, and after leaving Calgary, excitement mounted. It was evening when we topped the Kicking Horse Pass, but not much of British Columbia was seen, until by dawn we were running beside the turbulent Fraser River.

In Vancouver we were met by the man whose advertisement I'd seen and answered. He had booked rooms at an hotel which I had to refuse in favour of something much cheaper, and after giving us names and addresses which we might need, left us to it. The price of land, he said, had soared since last spring and though he'd made enquiries had decided I must go to various real estate agents, unless I decided, after all to get myself a job. The latter did not appeal at all for I wanted, above all, to get stuck into my own land, in my own way. But first, schools for the children had to be found, so that Myrah and I would be free to look for a property. There was nothing for it but boarding school, for no one, it seemed wished to have children as lodgers so that state schools could be used. With Bridget now twelve and Myrah's daughter aged eight at a girl's school, and Robert and Adrian, now nine and eight at a very British type boys' school, the way was clear, once I'd also bought a second-hand van and passed a driving test.

For three weeks, in an extra wet rainy season, we drove first inland and then over to Vancouver Island. Inland properties, for what they were, proved far too expensive. We were told that we'd have to go four or five hundred miles north into the hills to get the kind of property I kept enquiring for at the figure I told the various agents I had available — and I'd probably find no ready-made house to go with it. Most of the properties were small market gardens and though here and there I noted the land appeared to be good, I did not fancy setting up, after all these years free of market fluctuations, in that kind of business. Nor did I wish to begin again with purely nursery work with retail sales the most likely outlet, but with dubious chances of success.

On Vancouver Island it was the same story. Farms of fifty acres or more were quite out of reach — often remote and either impoverished or impossible for me to work alone. One such place, near Ladysmith, was of a hundred acres in a charming setting with a lake and woods. But the old wooden framehouse was near derelict, and there were acres where bed rock had little or no covering of soil. Another farm of a hundred and sixty acres had some potential and as always if worthwhile, I walked around with my spade, digging holes here and there to test the soil and what lay beneath it. I had to cross a creek and stumbling, dropped in up to my waist. I had mud up to my knees before emerging from the swamp beyond, and having lost my bearings in the falling darkness and rain I was glad at last to see the lights of the homestead. Again the price was out of reach, and it was only the offer of a mortgage from the owner that made me consider it at all. I consulted the Government Advisory Bureau in Victoria and though the officials were friendly and wanted to be helpful, there was so little they could do to help me. It was in fact, dawning on me that the chance of finding the kind of place I had built up in my mind was remote. Every other day relentlessly heavy rain made the search more frustrating, and as I drove north along the Island Highway to Courtenay, inspecting properties here and there, it seemed as if after all, I'd have to take one of the small places in the mainland — or get a job. Only the eastern coastal strip of the Island was worth considering. To the west was forest and mountain, where only logging was practiced. I was shown over a dreary upland where logged-off land could be bought for twenty dollars an acre — a thousand acres if you like, said the agent. But a house would have to be built and all these stumps would have to be cleared to free the thin rocky soil and then — what? Disheartened, there was still the Courtenay area to try. Up there the trees were tall and dense, but, cleared land was scarce, and just as expensive as elsewhere. I liked what I saw of the country and the sea glimpses, dotted with thickly forested islands with the mainland mountains showing fifty miles away, made me yearn to find somewhere where this search could after all find a happy conclusion.

This was disillusionment indeed, and as darkness fell and the rain came down once more, I had to turn south again towards Nanaimo for the ferry back to Vancouver. Half an hour later, the lights of the van picked up a wayside notice we'd not seen on the way up. "Waterfront house with 10 acres for sale", it said and an arrow pointed down a side road. It was a winding downhill track and it crossed what I knew to be the single C.P.R. line which ran from Victoria to north of Courtenay. Half a mile from the main highway, the lights shone on a new house in a clearing. A gaunt elderly man answered my knock. "It's just over there", he said, "belongs to my brother. He's the one who wants to sell."

Walter Pocock and his wife were at home in the one-storey wooden built house. He wanted to sell, he said, because in helping to build his brother Mont's new house, where we'd first called, he'd met with a serious accident and would be crippled for life, and must get back to Vancouver to live. Because of that, he was only asking 6,500 dollars in hopes of a quick sale, and if we'd care to stay the night so as to see around in daylight we'd be welcome, if we were potential buyers. Next morning the sun was shining and the sea, at the foot of the sloping cliff on which the house was built was sparkling. A little stream gurgled within sound of the room in which I slept. There was no electricity but water from a spring up there near the railway was piped down and it never failed. But for about a rood near the house the land had all been logged and, judging by the size of the stumps, some of the Douglas Firs must have been very high. A few bent saplings were standing, but the debris left by the loggers was appalling. Branches, rotten trunks and smashed down young trees were crissed crossed between the stumps so that walking was a matter of clambering. There were a few very dead trees still standing which Mr Pocock said were cedars. "Western Red Cedar", I thought though not cedars at all, but thuyas. He also gave them the name of "Widow Makers," because when dead they were dangerous to fell, even though the timber made good posts and rails for fencing.

With Myrah even more anxious than I to find a house, to put an end to this frustrating, nerve racking search, I paid Walter Pocock a deposit. The Island was an up and coming place he said, and this being a seaside property, we couldn't possibly go wrong. But for his disability for which he tended to blame his brother Mont, he'd have been content to stay. As it was we could come in as soon as we'd made arrangements to get the furniture out of storage and paid the rest of the money. Schooling for the children would be no problem because only half a mile away there was the Deep Bay State School where all the local children went.

A week later the big packing cases made from Bressingham wood arrived. With an annexe building a few yards away having two extra bedrooms in one of which I'd slept, there would be room for the four children. But having seen them back in Vancouver and described the new house, they were disappointed at being told they would have to stay in boarding school until Christmas, having paid a full term's fees, and needing time in which to make a home. But the first visit to Deep Bay was enough to make us realise that this was not the school for them, much as they disliked being boarders. It was a fishing village with one woman teacher for forty children of all ages and assorted races, and just would not do. This came as a blow, not only because I too would have preferred them to be with us, but because of the financial drain boarding school entailed.

But the die was cast, and again there was nothing for it but to make the best of a bad job. But for the demands on my time and energy, the anticlimax would have been intolerable. Myrah as companion housekeeper found life no more to her liking than before, as the wet dismal autumn turned to winter. Our only neighbours were Mont Pocock and his wife. He had been a forestry warden in Northern Manitoba and had come here to retire. They were a friendly, helpful couple, and seemed glad to have us as neighbours. Yet, without the children, there came a breach between Myrah and I which had appeared before, but which, now that her position was not subject to gossip, seemed to widen more than ever. We did not fight, for living our separate lives, there was nothing to fight about. She cooked and sewed and tended the house, and once a week we went together shopping in Courtenay.

Having taken to pieces all the furniture crates, Mont Pocock helped me to build a lean-to shed with the slats in which to keep firewood. This was one of the greatest bugbears. There was no dry firewood and the cookstove would not function well with the sodden logs I was able to cut up. I spent several days using a crosscut saw single handed on Douglas fir trunks, long since dead but resin rich. The rough terrain and steep slopes made this difficult, and I found it easier to handle chunks which on the steep slope had taken me up to an hour to saw through, and then roll them up the slope intact, to be split on the level since barrow wheeling was impossible. My work during that November when fourteen inches of rain was recorded, was mainly that of hewing wood and drawing water.

But the drawing of water was a case of being rid of water which saturated the patch of cleared land near the house, which was the only choice for a kitchen garden. The top soil was a reddish chestnut brown colour, containing some shale rock and of no great depth. I began the first drainage ditch on the top of the two hundred foot wooded cliff, for there was no other outlet for water on this side of the house. The little stream ran on the other boundary of the eighty yard wide oblong rectangle which was my property and, for most of its four hundred yards depth, there were no boundary posts or barriers.

Digging was easy at first, but at depths varying from one and a half to two and a half feet, I found a hard pan. It was not quite like solid rock, but a semi-petrified strata of small brown shale which needed a pickaxe to break through. Mostly it was three to four inches thick, but once through, drainage on both sides began to take place, as water found a way out.

Chapter Seven

DESPITE work and worry there were times when I took a breather to gaze over the sea, for when the sun shone it was very beautiful indeed. A wooded island lay only two miles away, and behind was the outline of the much larger Denman Island. This was the sea of a Thousand Islands which stretched all the way from Vancouver to Alaska, and to the north were the new snow covered peaks of the mainland coast which stood out on clear days. There were a few fishing boats coming in or out from Deep Bay and twice a week a C.P.R. steamer came past. From the house, the foreground and slope with its trees hid the beach itself, but there were log or boulder steps down to it. Down below there was nothing but rocks and logs. The latter had broken away from log rafts and cast up by the tide. Now and then one of these huge rafts of lashed tree trunks, on its way to the mill, was slowly towed by, behind a couple of noisy tugs. I guessed them to cover almost most of an acre in area, and were tended by men who stayed aboard in a little hut on the raft. Then there was also the twice daily sound of the C.P.R. locomotive, drawing its assortment of passenger and freight cars. Its whooping whistle could be heard miles away and the sound echoed through the trees as it passed once up, once down, only a few hundred yards away.

Such sights, natural or man-made, were so utterly unfamiliar that now and then I had to remind myself that I was in fact seeing the real thing and not a picture or cinema screen. It was not that there were too few reminders of reality, but as if a time shutter had clicked over the past months that led to my leaving England and that I had been so suddenly transported it was no more than an illusion. While it lasted, it was a queer sensation, and with the need to shake myself out of it and get back to work, I became less sure of the future and the objective of my labours. Certain factors began to stand out. The first of these was the necessity of making a living. Unless I cleared some more land, there was no prospect even of starting up a small nursery. But though the Island attracted holiday makers in summer from the mainland, the resident population was scanty, and few people seemed to bother much about gardening. Apart from fishing and lumbering there were no industries and the chance of getting a job was obviously remote.

For the present, I could do no other than carry on with ditch digging and clearing as large a patch of ground as time would allow for a garden. Mont Pocock had employed a bulldozer to clear his garden patch and it didn't worry him if a great pile of stumps was standing not far from his new house. He saw me making a fire one day, of useless dead wood where I decided to add a piece more ground to dig for garden space. To save cutting them through I was piling quite long pieces on to my fire criss cross fashion, but he said there was a better way. "Lay them all one way and they'll burn. I can see you're like I was forty years ago, fresh from the Old Country. It would be a sin over there to burn timber, but here there's so much you've got to get rid of it to clear the ground."

I soon found he was right. The fire took hold and as I laid on logs up to fifteen or eighteen feet long, all the same way, closely packed, it made within a hour a fire ten or twelve feet long and four feet high burning furiously. Mont showed me how to roll trunks as big as telegraph poles by artful leverage dodges to get them moved into position without having to lift them bodily. He had already lent me his cant hook which I'd found more than useful in moving trunks — logs in Canadian parlance — which would have been beyond my strength to budge. This was a strong pole with a hinged spike hook at the end which bit into the trunk to give leverage on it. Though brusque and dour of manner I liked him, and he often wandered over to chat, always willing to help whether help was needed or not. To hear of him telling of some of his experiences in Canada was as entertaining as reading Jack London's short stories.

December brought the first fall of snow. It was unusual, Mont said to have a severe winter on the Island, and if he was any judge, this meant that we might well be in for one this year. He was right and though much of the snow thawed, a hard frost set in, and well before Christmas the pipeline bringing water from the spring both to Mont's house and mine, froze up. We had been greatly troubled earlier on because the one indoor lavatory refused to function. I spent time dismantling the thing, both in the house and under it, trying to find out why the pan did not empty when the chain was pulled. It was more than inconvenient, and though I refrained from using it myself, I could not expect Myrah to do as I did, and find a secluded spot in the trees. Eventually the trouble was tracked down to a tin lid which the previous owners must have accidentally dropped down, as they were on the point of leaving, to make a blockage in the swan-neck after they'd gone.

But frozen supply pipes were a very different proposition. Mont and I began digging at the junction, near his gate, of his pipe line and mine. The gravel was frozen hard and though when we found the pipe it was free of frost at that point, there was nothing for it but to follow it up all the way until we came to where it was frozen. On this uneven surface, beside the track, it was at varying depths. Sometimes we had to make little tunnels under the rock-like frozen crust, which resisted even a sharp pickaxe, and after each stretch cover over again with mown bracken and grass to make insulation before soil was put back. At last we found the place where the pipe was only 9" deep and over this we lit a fire to thaw it out. Only a little water came and on we'd have to go again. It took us two weeks of hard work to free that pipe and make it safe, and then with Mont's water running ours stopped again. Somewhere in the eighty yards between his gate and our back door, this pipe too was frozen. Digging downward from Mont's took nearly another week, and at last I found the place — just where the pipe passed under the house and into the kitchen.

Such work had little relation to my anxieties for the future. It was something that had to be done in order to live with the present. With Christmas approaching the longing to have the children home made me count the days. Bridget and Philippa were due to break up a day earlier than Robert and Adrian. Myrah went with me to Nanaimo to meet them off the steamer, but I went alone next day to meet the boys. Fresh snow had fallen, and to get a better grip on the van tyres, I loaded in some rocks overnight. When I went to leave next morning, the extra weight had been too much for the wooden floor of the shed, and the back wheels had dropped through. It took an hour to jack up and back out. The steamer was gliding in as I arrived in Nanaimo but the boys were not on board. I telephoned to the school in Vancouver only to be told they would not be leaving until next day. And on the miserable fifty mile journey back to Deep Bay, a puncture had to come to cap it all.

The joy of having the children was offset by having to insist they went back for at least another term. But it had to be, and when they'd gone, future prospects became more stark, as I tried vainly to find a way of stemming the drain on my money resources. I could still gain some satisfaction from burning stumps and useless timber so long as I did not think too deeply about how profit could come from the meagre patch of land cleared by so doing. Mont said he heard sock-eye salmon were fetching a good price and that those trolling with a skiff out there in the channel were making it pay. Then, when I showed interest, he said he'd also heard that a skiff had been washed up about a mile along the beach, and the man who found it was willing to sell. Myrah came with me to bring it in. It was an old row-boat and needed repair. The oars were weak, but I managed to row it back, and by heaving rocks to one side, was able to beach it at high tide. Then from the Deep Bay Store, owned, as was the village itself by the Fishery Company, I bought trolling line, hooks and spinners. With Myrah at the tiller, game for any break in the monotony, I rowed out one calm day and let down the troll line. It was said to be eight hundred feet deep out there in the channel, and even with only a little knowledge of boats, I knew that we were taking considerable risks.

It was astonishing to look back to the shore. When there, nothing could be seen of the interior for trees, because there was rising ground back from the house. But now, half a mile or so away a quite unsuspected range of snow-covered mountains could be seen. Not more than four or five thousand feet perhaps, but till now, they had existed for me only on the map. I had to row slowly lest the half rotten oars snapped, and having gone out about a mile, I circled to return. Not a single tug came on the troll, and having headed the boat again I was glad it was still only on trial. It was not an option I wanted to take up and the six dollars I'd paid for the tackle was all I'd ever spend on fishing equipment there. A day or two later working again in sight of the sea, I saw some dark shapes out there where we'd been. I shouted to Mont splitting firewood near his house, and he joined me. "Killer whales," he explained in his casual way. "I've seen 'em several times like that — twenty or thirty come by, in and out, squirting water. Fishermen keep on the look out and get out of their way, sure thing. I forgot to tell you about those durned beasts when you were going out the other day." I admitted that had he done so, I doubt if I'd have gone, and then he came out with something else that brought a ray of hope. There was to be a new Island Highway to replace the old, which was atrociously bad. "And the Surveyor told me himself that it's coming well this side of the old road. They're taking an acre or more of my land and I reckon it will be within yards of yours. They're sure to need fence posts, so if you want another job while the frost lasts, why not fell those two dead cedars over there, and cut them up? They'd give you a nickel each for posts — but be careful — they're not called widow makers for nothing."

The trunk of the first one was so widely splayed out at the base that I had to rig up a platform five feet high before I could begin to fell it. My double bedder axe was sharp, but the wood was hard, and it took nearly all day to fell it alone. Mont came down to advise me once or twice but kept well clear, and having driven in wedges to cant it over, at last the eighty foot tree crashed down. Using the cross cut was easier now, and having cut through the first eight foot length I used wedges again for splitting. Apart from the larger knots it was a fairly simple matter to rive out posts of the required thickness. This stuff would, in fact, split down into infinitely thin pieces, like pipe lighters or spills if desired, pinging cleanly away from the main piece with fascinating precision. But I was after as many posts as I could get in the shortest space of time, and though it took me a week to reduce the tree, I reckoned there would be twenty-five dollars worth at least, when the time came to sell them.

Then, late in February, the frost gave way and the snow melted. By early March I was able to dig once more, and with spade and fork, turned over what would now be a sizeable garden. Part of it I would use for vegetables, but the rest would make the beginnings of a nursery for I'd had word to say that a consignment of plants I'd ordered to be sent from Bressingham was on its way. It was during March that Mont said he'd met the foreman in charge of the new highway. Work had already begun and he was looking for more labour. If I could persuade him to let me take a section or two close to home at piece work rates for clearing trees, I might earn some useful money, if I'd a mind to.

I found Bill Eddy, the road contractor's site manager, about three miles away, swearing profusely at a bunch of men building a fire of stumps and branches, which a bulldozer was pushing in. He was a lanky man of about fifty, and as he let rip at the men's inefficiency despite liberal use of fuel oil, I waited a few yards away, hoping I'd not chosen an unpropitious moment to put the question, "Any chance of a job?" to him. I'd had that question put to me often enough in the past, and whilst waiting could not help an inner snigger at the thought that for the first time ever, I'd come to the position of having to use it myself. Less than a year ago I was the boss for thirty to forty men, and the one to say "yes" or "no" to such a question from others. Bill Eddy looked my way and I came nearer with — "Any chance of a job?" He eyed me up and down with a scowl and then said, "You're a goddam Britisher ain't you?"

I nodded and grinned. "But I can work," I added.

"Now! — I never met a Britisher yet who had guts enough to work — on this sort of job anyway. Too soft. No-siree, I ain't got no work for you."

I'd been afraid of this and came out with an offer to work for a day or two to prove myself. If he then thought I was no good, he needn't pay me. That made him eye me up and down once more, with a surprised look. "Hell's bells — that's the first time a guy has said that to me when he's asked for a job. That's a fair offer — but can you use an axe and make a fire?"

A few minutes later, he was following me in his pick-up back to the Deep Bay turning, and having been shown the blaze marks in the woods by Mont where the new highway crossed it, I told Bill Eddy that this was where I'd like to take on a section or two, at piece work. These sections were marked out by blazes cut in the bark of trees, roughly a hundred feet by a hundred feet, and there must be, I reckoned, close on a hundred trees of all sizes growing in each section — Douglas fir, hemlock, cedar, pine and alder, with a carpet of Salmon berry below. All I had to do, said Bill Eddy, was to cut them down and burn them. The D.4 Caterpillar bulldozer would push out and pile up the stumps.

Having done a day's work I reckoned thirty dollars a section would be a fair price — basing it on a dollar an hour. It was accepted without argument from Bill Eddy who by the end of my first week was becoming an embarrassment. I told him on the third day when he came to see me that I didn't care for beer, but still he persisted, trying to get me to take a break and share the beer he took round in his truck with him. So as to avoid offence I asked him in one evening for a meal for which he brought beer for himself and wine for Myrah and me, and after that he was more attentive than ever.

During the next few weeks I cleared and burnt up five sections and then took a break for Easter, with the children home again. The four cases of plants arrived from Bressingham, having taken six weeks en route, and though many had died or suffered it was surprising, after such a time, how many were still alive. But as I unpacked, planted and labelled, the futility of it all struck home. Money was dwindling so fast that something drastic had to be done, and when Bill Eddy offered me the job of foreman on the new highway scheme, provided I could stick with him for an even bigger contract to follow it on the mainland, I found it very tempting. One by one my illusions had been shattered, and I had to chose one of three alternatives. To go on contract work with Bill Eddy might bring enough money to keep us somewhere in British Columbia, but for much of the time I would be away from home. To cut my losses and go back to England was no way out for me — to admit I was licked and defeated after only a few months. I'd made a mistake in coming to the west coast because unless I got a job I couldn't make a living. But a friendly agent in Nanaimo had recently moved from Southern Ontario where, he said, farms were quite cheap to buy. This brought on the idea of making the trip east, and whilst checking up on properties for sale, call on nurserymen both there and in the U.S.A. to obtain export orders for Bressingham. The more I thought about it the more hopeful I became, and when I decided to go Myrah was all for it, provided I did not leave her behind.

With the van sold there was just enough money with my wages from Bill Eddy to pay for the trip. We took the Canadian National Railway this time on its more northerly route via Jasper and Edmonton, and arrived in Toronto in mid-May, to find it an un-lovely, unfriendly city by the time I'd scouted around for information. I bought a 1938 Nash car from a man advertising privately, since Mont had advised me to keep away from dealers. Good advice no doubt, but I was mug enough to believe the man when he said the low oil pressure reading was due to the need for a refill with new oil. He gave me the most solemn assurances. Being in a hurry I paid him the six hundred dollars, so as to get out of Toronto as soon as possible, and because the car had let down seats to make a bed for Myrah and with me using the little tent we'd brought over, it would at least save dollars in lodgings. An oil change for the Nash on the Queen's Highway to the southwest soon proved the measure of the seller's solemn word of honour. The pressure stayed so low that I wondered what trouble lay in wait somewhere on the four to five thousand mile trip I was intending to take. But at least it was smooth riding, which was more than could be said for the one ton van I had had in British Columbia.

I called at nurseries, wherever I could, in the hope of booking orders. It was the rush season for them, with their short spring nearly over, and where owners or managers were not too busy to see me, others said they preferred to buy from Holland. We went down

(xvi)   The River Waveney at Bressingham in 1947 which places the land on the Norfolk/Suffolk border.

(xvii)   The floods of March, 1947, after clearing bushes during the preceding frost.

(xviii)   Harvesting the old way at Bressingham in 1947.

(xix)   A stack yard in 1947 but the Railway Museum Yard to-day.

(xx)　Chalky water being pumped from the new bore hole at Bressingham.

(xxi)　These spruce trees blew down during the winter of 1947. The timber was used to make packing cases for furniture being shipped to Canada.

(xxii)   Myrah inspecting the furniture when it arrived in Deep Bay, Vancouver Island, Canada from England. The Author inspects the Bressingham spruce cases which he made into a shed

(xxiii)   Another challenge. The land in Canada the Author began to clear in October 1948.

(xiv)   A view (left) from the house on Vancouver Island and (right) Bridget, Robert, Adrian and Myrah's daughter, Philippa, at Keep Bay half a mile from the house.

(xxv)   Back at Bressingham from Canada. A view before making the garden.

(xxvi)   A new pond under construction in 1955.

(xxvii)   The pond fifteen years later.

(xviii)   A bridge built about 1957 for the cattle to cross becomes a feature as the garden develops.

(xxix)   A pool is built as part of the 1958 garden making.

(xxx)   The first stage in making a sunken bed.

(xxxi)   The second stage with the Author building the wall.

to Hamilton and along the Lake Erie shore, and by that time I'd had enough of being a representative. I was never much good with sales talk, and I was none too sure what the Bressingham nursery was in a position to supply. I turned north, through Guelph and beyond, making a wide arc past Lake Simcoe on the look out for small farms for sale. The countryside did not appeal until, skirting the wooded Halliburton country, we came south again via Fenelon Falls into Peterborough, having covered nearly a thousand miles, all in Southern Ontario.

This area was more to my liking and enquiries became more intensive. We looked at several farms in the hilly country to the west of Peterborough, and true enough, land was much cheaper here and the houses were mostly brick built and solid. One farm of a hundred acres near Cavan attracted me. It was on a southern slope with a spring for water and a sizeable creek at the wooded bottom of the valley. It possessed the only gravel pit in the district, said the owner who was leaving because his wife wanted to go back to live in town. I walked over it, digging occasional holes and came back to see if I could shift the owner from his asking price of $6,500.

The ray of hope I was following now was that of finding a place in Southern Ontario where I could combine farming with a distribution centre for British grown nursery stock. This idea had come with the realisation that there was no future for me in British Columbia, but within a few hundred miles were large and prosperous cities, especially across the border in the U.S.A. Nurserymen to whom I had mooted the proposal were favourably disposed, saying that if I could supply their needs and meet Dutch competition, they'd certainly be interested, and would prefer to buy British. But the need to find a base was becoming acute. We'd had three weeks travelling and though most of the scenery and weather was pleasant enough, it had been anything but a holiday. Myrah was sometimes frantic, sometimes quite poorly, from mosquito bites which were an immediate menace with any break in the journey and especially when camping at night.

It was a temptation to do a deal for that farm of a hundred acres, at the same price paid for the ten acres at Deep Bay, because the land was potentially fertile and some peaty swamp near the creek only needed a ditch or two for drainage. At this figure it was dearer than some I'd seen, but saying I'd let the owner know next day, one way or the other, I decided I must do some calculations to gauge whether or not I would have funds enough. Just for a check I called in at a gateway half a mile away with a red brick house which was quite close to the dusty road. An elderly man and a younger woman were walking to the big red barn from the house when I asked if they'd do me a favour.

I explained the reason for my call, and was soon told that both the farm and its owners had a bad name. "Four owners in ten years," said Mr Sissons — the name on the mail box by the gate. "We'd sell you this one for a lot less than he's asking," put in his wife. "Our hundred acres is as good as his".

Three hours later I wrote out a check for $200 deposit. It was all I could manage, and the Sissons were quite content with my explanation of having to sell up at Deep Bay and to pay for the move which we agreed should take place in July, six weeks hence. Bruce Sissons had only just decided to retire and was about to put the farm on the market, so it seemed that at last, luck had changed for us. They had walked over the farm with us, every field, down the steep slope on the one side, to the swamp and creek, up through woods and a rock strewn lane. Rocks were mostly rounded granite, obviously brought here by glaciation, and if crops were not heavy, the grass was green and, surely, I ought to be able to make a living. Even if a distribution base for nursery stock took time to develop, I could find plenty of scope for improvements to the property.

The most pressing need was to have the Nash put right for the long journey back by road. The small deposit on the farm allowed about $50 for this and by going into upstate New York first, there I hoped to collect the 300 dollars owed by a big nursery at Newark, for a consignment of plants sent from Oakington in 1939, which had never been paid for. That or even half the debt, would see us through, and make it possible to call on some other American nurseries too, on the way to Seattle. This had to be the route, for there was no highway through Canada's middle west, and to go north of the Great Lakes would be much further anyway.

I took the car into a Nash agency garage, and the manager confirmed my worst fears. The bearings and crankshaft would have to be renewed to make a job of it and that would cost a lot of money. There was no cheaper way out, and when I asked him for a straight answer on the chances of getting to Seattle without a serious breakdown he said it would be two to one against and then only if I kept the oil sump full and kept the speed down to 40 m.p.h. There was no option but to take the risk, and with the usual grins and raised eyebrows because Myrah and I were travelling together with different names and passports, we passed through the U.S. Customs at Niagara Falls into U.S.A. Had Myrah not been attractive looking to the male eye, no doubt this kind of embarrassment would not have occurred — and many others, since I myself was first so attracted four years before.

By now, we were on speaking terms only. There was a bond of mutual need for children, home making, and what security could be found, but being thrown together so much ever since we came to Canada had not brought us closer in spirit. She waited nearly two hours in the car whilst I waited to see the head of the nursery in Newark, N.Y., south of Lake Ontario. When I rejoined her I had good reason to look both glum and grim. He had repudiated the debt, and there was nothing for it but to head west as quickly as the Nash bearings would allow, and as cheaply as we could make it. Although I called at one nursery at Mentor, Ohio, where bills had been promptly paid, I could not bring myself to ask for a loan on account of future orders. Two other firms on the way beyond were closed, one for a Sunday, the other for a general holiday.

Chapter Eight

THAT journey, from Newark to Seattle, took eleven days for the three thousand odd miles, keeping below forty and nursing the engine like a frail horse. Through the flat farm lands of Indiana, Illinois and Iowa it was dreary travelling and camping sites were hard to find. Nebraska's rolling hills, with the dead straight road visible over the next hill but one, was not much better until the wilder bluff country, and in Jersey National Park, we even paused to look at the wild flowers. Across Wyoming along the Wind River Canyon we smelt and tasted the hot springs at Thermopolis. That evening at dusk we were on a high wild moor with sixty miles to go to the next township. I backed off the road leaving Myrah to make up her bed, as I tried to put up my tent against the strong wind. Myrah had protested at staying in such a spot, and I'd become cussed with toothache. She had a hacking cough, and I was at heart sorry for her. With the tent up the primus would not go because of the gale, and when Myrah broke down, becoming almost hysterical, I gave in. There wasn't really any danger that the car would take off during the night down the slope and into a ravine down there but . . .

At midnight we reached a Motel at Cody with Myrah sure she had bronchitis. I slept in the car for a change and she in a room. We stayed the next night and half a day in Yellowstone Park and saw the sights and then on again. Myrah began to feel better as we came down from the Rockies, but my only complaint was the aching tooth, apart from having to keep the hunger at bay with flat cakes and bran muffins day after day. The rest of the journey was more interesting, geographically, but financially very stringent indeed. Through Idaho and the dry belt beyond where the Colombia was harnessed for irrigation so effectively it was good to climb into the cool greenery of the Coast Range mountains and above all to drift down to Seattle with the Nash making no more inner rattlings than she'd done all along. From Seattle we took the night ferry to Victoria on Vancouver Island, and with only one silver dollar left of American money, I kept this as a souvenir. A tickling cough bothered me as we left Victoria by the Island Highway, and it lasted the hundred and thirty miles to Deep Bay, tiringly incessant. Tired out, we slept the clock round that night, and next morning not even the view across the sea brought a qualm that we might, in moving, be going from the frying pan into the fire. After all, the change of luck had held, and as I pressed the starter button of the Nash to go down to the Deep Bay store for supplies, the engine fired first time.

Mont said he'd be sorry to see us go, but felt sure we were doing the right thing. He offered to keep an eye on the place if by the time we left it no buyer had come along. That left a month and though I said I'd be content to get back the $6,500 I'd paid for it, and throw in what improvements I'd made, such as the garden, which was looking quite attractive now, Mont had doubts. The post war property boom, he said, had slackened and prices had fallen. He'd do his best, but I was not to be surprised if it took longer than a month to sell for my figure. This was rather a damper, for it was on the strength of a ready sale that I was relying for the necessary funds with which to pay Bruce Sissons back in Cavan, Ontario.

There was much to do, and tidying up the garden had to take second place to giving the house a quick coat of paint and making arrangements to move. The children were due home for summer vacation and loading the furniture into a freight van at Bowser station and making it secure for the three thousand mile journey, would be a lengthy task. I had more than merely toyed with the idea of doing a deal with the Nash in exchange for a truck on which the furniture could all be packed, since the C.P.R. asked what I thought a stiff figure for rail transport. For reasons of her own, though no doubt with my welfare also in mind, Myrah was dead against it. I certainly did not relish the thought of such a journey, but money was very tight, and credit was non-existent. But just in time, a remittance from England arrived and I decided to go ahead by rail, with the furniture to be sent in advance by freight train.

The children were overjoyed at being home, and with the news that they would not again be sent away to school. But it was scarcely the holidays they'd been hoping for of playing in the woods or on the beach below. The girls helped Myrah to pack whilst the boys helped me. Having ordered an empty freight car I was dismayed when I saw it standing at Bowser station four miles away, to find that on its last trip it had carried coal. It took much of one day for us to sweep the dust out, and even then we were not sure that some might still be lurking in joints and partitions. A local lorry owner brought a load each morning, and with battens, screws, nails and hammer plus lengths of rope, we packed in all the furniture—including some rather fine antique stuff I'd accumulated over the years, so that after five day's work all was as safe as we could make it. There was no limit, I'd been warned, to the rough handling freight cars received on such a journey. Not, "get there or bust," but "get there and bust" was the motto the rail men went by.

For a few nights we had to use sleeping bags on the floor, and the last meal or two Mrs Pocock was kind enough to provide with Myrah's help. Since the beginning of 1949 the friendly steam engine on the nearby line had gone and in its place had come a diesel to haul the daily mixed train. By arrangement on the morning we left, it stopped where the Deep Bay road crossed the tracks and the six of us, with our great pile of luggage went aboard for Nanaimo and over to Vancouver once more. There we took the evening train eastwards for Toronto, arriving there four days later in a heat wave. Such humidity, due to the Lake, it was said, was almost overwhelming, and we were glad to be out of the city and to be in the country once more, seventy miles to the north east, on a secondary C.P.R. line to Peterborough and Ottawa. At Cavan station two friendly neighbours whom we'd met after doing the deal earlier with Bruce Sissons were there, Leslie Pritchard and Herb Morton farmed on either side, and one lent tractor and trailer for luggage, whilst the other drove us to the farm by car.

It was less unpleasantly hot up there on the hill, but the signs of drought which I'd noticed before reaching Toronto were just as evident here. In place of the lush greenery of late May, now, in the third week of July, all was parched. Les and Herb said this was nothing unusual and I reflected that here, well south of the forty-ninth parallel, summers were bound to be hot. Thunder storms they also said had been much fewer this year than usual, but they would come sure enough and houses and barns were not fitted with lightning conductors for nothing, they added reassuringly. When we walked over the farm that evening, I was dismayed at the poverty of the grain crops. Only twenty five acres had been sown, and with the pastures brown with drought, I saw my old enemy—drought—staring me once more in the face with menacing challenge. And Myrah again attacked by her special enemy, the mosquito.

We slept on the floor of the empty house for nearly three weeks before finally the freight car with furniture caught up. Down at Cavan station came another shock, for despite all the trouble we had taken piece after piece was damaged, and every drawer, every surface and crevice was black with fine coal dust. By the time the furniture was mended, cleaned and placed in the house, shelves and cupboards fitted, a sweaty week had passed. The Sissons had not, as promised, emptied the earth closet. The one father had dug out at Over in 1921 would have lasted the Sissons a long time, but theirs was full to the hole and we could not use it. Instead I rigged up an Elsan type in an outhouse, and I had to dig holes for emptying this twice in the first week.

The Sissons had also said that the well, on a patch of rough grass in front of the house, had never been known to run dry. They knew the previous owners, who also declared it had never failed. But two weeks after we came, the pump failed to bring up the third of three buckets full I'd been asked to draw so that the girls could have a stand up bath in the tin wash tub we had. There was no indoor water, but I'd meant to rig up an indoor pump from the well to a tank upstairs as the very next job in order of importance. I took off the lid and saw only the glimmer of water in the bottom. A weight on a string showed it to be three inches deep at a depth of fifteen feet, and I saw too, the desperate situation this revealed. There were protests from the others when I said I was going down to try and deepen it. The well walls were built of granite boulders, and the dislodgement of one could easily bring many more down which could be more than embarrassing for someone at the bottom. But someone had to go down, and I had to reduce protests to an ultimatum.

It was only about two feet across inside, and as I gingerly went down the ladder my shoulders touched those menacing rocks. At the bottom it was more cramped still, and I found a foot or more of mud that must be taken out. Robert, strong for his age, hauled up a few buckets on a rope which I'd half filled. Each time he emptied it he called down to me to announce what he'd found in the mud—a broken jug, an old shoe, some bones and pieces of glass. At the end of an hour, I'd come to solid bottom and was thankful to be on solid earth above once more, with the realisation that, apart from any reluctance to drink water from that well because of what foulness the mud had contained, there would not be enough for household use anyway.

So little water had come in to the well as a result of my deepening efforts that until I found a better supply somewhere else, water would have to be brought up the hill from a spring which rose a hundred and fifty yards away below the barn. I'd already tasted that and decided that it was far enough away from an old muck heap not to be contaminated. This, I thought would be the place for a much less deep well, to supply water for the house.

On the strength of hoping to sell the Island property, I had to keep my promise to Myrah that in moving to Cavan, where there was electricity, she should have a cooker and fridge, and bathroom with W.C. The cooker and fridge were delivered and fitted on the day the water supply failed, and for the first time ever, I had to go in for hire purchase in order to get them. Both were badly needed, for the oil stove the Sissons had used was worn out and smelly, and in that climate, food did not keep at all well in the outhouse known as the "summer kitchen". But indoor water was also desperately needed, and though I fixed the bath in position, water had to be carried in by buckets.

I judged the fall from the house to the spring from which I carried water to be about twenty feet, though it was over a hundred yards distant across the slope. To take a spirit-level reading would have been difficult because of humps and obstructions and knowing that the maximum lift for a mechanical pump was twenty five feet, I had to take a chance. Building a little well to trap the spring was a pleasant job on a hot day. The water was cool and there were plenty of rocks to use for walls. With water level well up to surface I began my trench for the pipe in as direct a line as possible to the house, shallow at first and then three and a half feet deep to keep it frost free. It was sweaty work in the hard dry ground, abounding in rocks of all sizes, some so large that I had to by pass a tunnel under them. The children, free and easy at last roamed the farm, making wigwams and playing cowboys and Indians. The current pop song was "Cruising down the River", and the tune stuck in my head as I laboured, and I laughingly let them know it jarred with me, with such words at such a time. But as a joke it soon grew stale for me when thereafter they teased me with it as they passed by.

It was a little cooler by the time I reached the house, having laid in nearly three hundred feet of inch and a quarter secondhand piping I'd brought from Peterborough. I dug under the raised "summer kitchen" and into the cellar under the house itself where the electric pump was already fixed. I connected up the pipe and after priming with water went back several times to the spring to seal the suction valve. For some reason, this vital non-return valve, designed to keep the pipe full of water and prevent an air lock, was defective. For most of one day I carried buckets of water from the spring well back to the new pump for priming, only to find it was steadily running back through the pipe to the well. At last I made it hold, and then pressing the switch, believed our water troubles would at last be over. But scarcely a kettleful came out of the tap in the room above. And another day was spent, on priming and trying again and again until the man who had supplied the pump came in response to my call over the party telephone line, which the Sissons had left for us.

"I'd say it's not the fault of the pump," were his first remarks. He cast his eye over the still open trench to the spring and then walked over to it and cast his eye back to the house. "I'll get that fall checked this afternoon with my level — I'm pretty certain that's your trouble." It was. His level showed a drop of twenty nine feet and showed too, the inaccuracy of my judgement, the only excuse for which was my being unused to dealing with sloping ground. It was a blow to my pride as I then laboured to unscrew all the piping and fill in the trench, as daily the need for water became more acute and somehow, more of a reproach to me.

Pondering glumly, I decided that there was a chance that the spring might be tapped higher up — in what went for a kitchen garden on the same level as the house and the big barn in the meadow beyond. There was a slight dip in the surface and there, thirty or forty yards away, I dug a test hole. If I found water or even traces of it at the maximum depth from which I could throw up the soil, it would be worth making into a new well. I dug, in a cramped space, through top soil, brown gravelly subsoil with glacial rocks, but at about nine feet I had to give up. It was almost as dry down there as on top.

Next I tried just below the house on a rough grassy patch, making sure that this time levels were registered first. This too was a test hole and also produced nothing but a dampish clay at eight or nine feet deep. With harvest time, I had to break off. Herb Morton and Les Pritchard helped one another at harvest time, and since I had no implements or machinery, it was the least I could do to offer my labour in helping in their harvest in return for their help, with mine. The sheaves were all stacked inside their respective barns, and if it was hot work out in the fields, stooking or carting, it was hotter still stacking under a barn roof. Belated, but very welcome, a violent storm broke just as harvest ended in mid-August. I do not, like some, revel in thunder and lightning. If it had not been for the welcome rain—the first we'd seen—it would have been quite frightening, for I'd never experienced anything like it and it lasted for most of one night so incessantly that I did not even undress for bed.

Both neighbours grinned widely and made the "What did I tell you?" remark about the storm, but accepted the rain as a godsend, saying that the next job now would be dung carting and spreading from the great pile accumulated near their barns. They were both traditional farmers, whose forebears several generations before had settled this land, in an area where Protestant Irish predominated and where Orange Day was still celebrated. I liked the earthy humour of Les and Herb, and though we heard of English immigrants who did not mix, we seemed to be accepted and sometimes others how passed by called in for a chat. One passer by said he was from the little township of Millbrook five miles away, and had heard that we were having trouble in finding water. He was, he said, a diviner and soon brought out his forked stick and began walking with it held in the usual way, round the house. Neither of my two test holes pulled the stick down and I was rather sceptical of the whole performance even if it offered a slight renewal of hope. The original well too was dismissed as of no account with the remark that if it hadn't ever given out before it was because the occupants didn't use much water.

After a few circles, he came back to the house and tried closer in and as we watched from the steps of the summer kitchen, the stick went down sharply when he was only a few paces away, on the same level as the house. "Here's the spot," he called gleefully. "Just where a well should be, and if you dig here you'll find oodles of water and not very deep either." I asked him how deep. "Not very deep, I tell you—under twenty feet, well under, I'd say." This was exciting, and hope came rushing back. The man refused payment and said he was only too glad to be of service. He'd helped dozens in his time and had never charged a cent—it was a gift to him and he'd pass on the benefit.

This was a Saturday evening, and on the Sunday morning I began digging with a will. This would be a proper well, and I made it six feet across at the top, intending to leave a ledge at eight or nine feet so that if I had to go twice that depth, I could lay a platform over half the hole, and throw up the soil in stages. After the rain digging was easier and as if to bless this final attempt, there were no rocks I could not handle alone. I came to a hard packed clay at eight feet, and then left a ledge. That clay layer was so hard that neither fork nor spade would penetrate and I had to borrow a mattock. With this I managed to pare off flakes, like parings of cheese, and gained only four feet more depth for four day's work. Three feet lower it was softer, and then came more gravel. This, I thought was unusual, because I'd never known of gravel underlying clay in England. But this was a glaciated country and hopes rose because this seam of gravel could well be water bearing and so prove the dowser's prediction correct. That gravel seam proved to be six or seven feet thick, and sandy and stony by turn, but hope turned to misgiving when I came once more to clay. Throwing it up on to the platform above my head and then going up myself to throw it again on top was slow work.

From then on, I had to press Robert and Adrian to help, with equal reluctance on both sides but from different standpoints. I rigged up a pulley and tripod, and with me at the bottom filling buckets, and Robert on the platform above me pulling the rope to raise a full one as one came down which Adrian had emptied, we eventually got down to twenty-two feet. Robert had to stand on an old chair placed on the platform to help him reach. Once there was a rumble on the boards, and suspecting the boys were larking I peered up the opening from below just as Robert toppled over. The chair hit me first on the head and then Rob, all arms and legs. It took us a minute or two to sort ourselves out lying there together on the bottom, winded, but only bruised. The soil was still clay, but with a difference. There was both moisture and fine sand in it, and this spelt danger. The sides began slowly to cave in, slipping downwards and inwards to where I lay. Treading it like dough under my feet, I found I was slipping and sending up far more than the actual width of the well, and when what would have filled two barrows flopped down, I knew that tactics had to be changed. A large wooden tub lay in the barn and this I let down the well, after knocking out the bottom. The staves would be some safeguard, I thought, but just then the boys had to begin school, which was half a mile down the road at Cavan.

The dowser called again, just as my hopes had dwindled to almost zero. "Don't give up — it's there O.K. — oodles of it," he said, but peering down he could see the problem — and the danger was with the bottom six feet of the well becoming bulbous, in shape. He said that what I needed was a sand point — a strong three inch pipe to which a point was fitted and above this some holes, so that by driving it in to penetrate this clay stuff, water below it would seep into the holes and could then be pumped direct.

A trip to Peterborough produced a sandpoint and by using a screw-on nipple to protect the thread, I began driving it in from the platform by pulling up a heavy lump of oak over the pulley and letting it act as a hammer. All very ingenious, I thought, until I found how difficult it was to let the weight fall so that the sandpoint pipe was hit squarely. On and off, I spent a couple of days on it, trying what variations I could, but at the end of it, I reckoned that, allowing for depth below surface of the pump in the cellar, the total lift would be over twenty-five feet. Even if I succeeded in driving the sandpoint any deeper, and found water, it would again be beyond the capacity of the pump to suck it up.

I was beaten. To reflect on how much pleasure I gained as a boy from digging holes for no real purpose was no comfort now. Nor was it to survey that huge heap of spoil so near, every time I went in and out of the house, spoil which had been moved two or three times already, had sooner or later to be moved again — back in the hole where the sandpoint was stuck so fast that I could not pull it out. I could blame the dowser, but saw the futility of this because I'd placed no faith in him at the outset, and he'd only believed he could help.

*   *

September was hot. I'd helped Herb with his barn dung for a week then felt like having a change. The spring from which I still drew water for the house was not the only one on the farm. Another across the far side of the same eight acre meadow was also too far down the slope. It made a little creek and joined with the nearer spring creek almost at the valley bottom to make a swamp of several acres. Here the soil was peaty — 'muck land' they called it. All it needed was a drainage ditch around its upper side perimeter to catch the spring and seepage water and lead it to the main creek — a little river in the valley bottom. We'd bathed and paddled in this, but had to have bare skin protected by rolled and tied on newspapers against mosquitos which were extra fierce down there. I'd caught suckers very easily and Myrah, with some reluctance, had cooked them, but this method of saving money was not repeated for they were boney tasteless fish. Money was very short indeed and devaluation by the British Labour Government had cut my vital remittance from Bressingham considerably. It would have been just enough to live on at Cavan, with no school fees to pay, but for this cut. Now once more I saw the need to earn wages, though the chances in that area were slim. In the darkening evenings and well into the night I answered several "Situations Vacant" advertisements and wrote a series of articles and a few short stories, but could find no sale for them.

I began the ditch designed to drain the swamp, partly as a change, because instead of digging to find water, it was digging to let it run away. Without much real hope I thought of improving the property and cultivating the swamp to plant up with nursery stock which would become saleable, but though there was some relief and some enjoyment in this preparatory task, the more my ditch extended, the more remote its objectives became. After fifty yards or so having dug six feet wide and four feet deep with a steady run of water in the bottom. I decided that the problem of water for the house really must come first.

Herb Morton's land began one field over to the west, abutting as did mine against the dusty gravel road known postally as RR1. His house was much further down from the road than ours and the slope was gentler. He had no real water problem because a little creek rising in a spongy area near the road trickled down the slope to keep his domestic well supplied. Knowing our need, he said if I cared to tap this supply at the source, he would have no objection and reckoned there was a slight fall from there to our house, three hundred yards distant. After prospecting it, all the way with a straight-edge board and spirit level, I decided there was just enough fall. But to dig a trench three hundred yards long, three and a half feet deep, and to bury the needful piping was not a project I dare rush into. Besides, I had just bought a cow and this was giving more trouble than the milk was worth.

Till then, milk had been fetched daily from Herb Morton—a chore the children took by turns. Myrah had often said we ought to have a cow, now that green grass had come and we had a supply of hay, but I'd been rather against it because of the outlay. But just down the road a farmer with a herd of Jerseys was selling up, and I went to the auction on the chance of a bargain. I poked in a bid here and there as the cows came into the ring, and then when the last one came something drove me to bid again till it was knocked down to me for $120. I'd have felt I'd failed somehow in a duty to the family had I not bought a cow, but in trying to drive it home against its will, away from its herd, I was soon wishing I'd stayed away from the auction. It ran wild and when finally inside the meadow gate it began to bellow and bellowed day and night for a fortnight. I tried and failed miserably to milk her, but even that was only after the boys and I had driven her into a corner and tied her up. They had a go, and because they met with some success, it became their twice daily job. But it needed all three of us, twice a day, to corner her and tie her up for milking. On more than one occasion she broke loose, and we had to chase her all over again when baiting was disdained. She was a proud, haughty and temperamental cow, with a knack of suddenly turning about face when being driven and charging with head down. It was no joke, and much as we tried to make a joke of it, because she was pining for her relations in the now dispersed herd, she ate little and gave very little milk. Adrian, only nine years old, and Rob a year older, secretly joined with me in hating the sight and sound of her, and the demands she made on us for the sake of the half a gallon of milk she gave. Once, bringing in the milk needed for breakfast, Adrian stumbled as he carried the bucket up the steps into the summer kitchen and spilt the lot. When chided for clumsiness he broke down and I wished I could have given him a hug and said comforting words. I was not the only one for whom life had become hard, infinitely harder than that which we had forsaken at Bressingham just a year ago. Nor was I in any position to complain, and though no complaints came from the children — they knew things were tight and if sometimes I had to be hard, I believed they understood. Myrah's complaints were mainly on the score of water and the smelly waterless closet, and though she fed us as well as money would allow, and kept what fears she had mainly to herself, the breach between us had widened.

The search for more second-hand piping led to five hundred feet being delivered, without which I was reluctant to begin the new trench. It was bought from the sale of the grain from the farm. The threshing machine and some helpful neighbours came one morning, and by late evening the whole lot was in sacks. It was for me the most gruelling day's work ever, for it was threshed inside the barn. By custom the farmer whose harvest was being threshed on this neighbour-help basis, took the worst job — that of piling up the straw. The thresher used worked at a furious rate, mangling and chopping the straw which was blown out from the tail end of the drum. The noise was deafening and the dust and heat were stifling. Even with a cloth tied over my mouth and nose when a pause came for a drink I coughed with blood flecks from my lungs and throat, and before the hellish task ended I began to fret lest serious damage was done.

From this, trench digging again came as a pleasant task, and though it might take weeks for completion final success was this time assured. I began at the corner of the house, just outside the cellar on the opposite side from the still gaping, still almost dry twenty-four foot well. There was a rise of about three feet to the other side, and keeping to three and a half feet depth would not have been hard digging, but for rocks, which if too large to heave or lever out, had to be tunnelled under or bypassed. At the far side I dug a small well, four or five feet deep. It was about half-way from the spring area, and having learned the hard way at Burwell that unless there is a good fall friction within a small bore pipe over a long distance will impede if not prevent a flow, the little well was to serve as a kind of booster. By letting water build up inside, the friction factor would be broken, and it could enter the second stage with renewed impetus. It was an idea that had occurred with this factor in mind, and I felt rather pleased with myself as a result.

It took three weeks to reach the spring and another week to lay and screw the piping. In the boggy spring area, I had to dig a boxed in catch pit that would not become fouled with mud, to draw the water from the gravel below the mud. Then came the great moment, with pipe fixed, water ran into the half-way well, filled it up and then entered the second length of a hundred and fifty yards to the house. There the final connection was made, and at last, ever-running water was on tap inside the house. And it was late October, with the first cold snap arriving to bring rich colours to the maples and oaks. But it was not quite the last of my diggings. Below the old earth closet the Sissons had left, I dug a septic tank, and laid drain pipes to it from the house and some more away from it to take the seepage. With the wind right, I then set light to the hut, and added the spoil from my septic tank pit to cover over the site. In early November came the Indian summer which, from a climatic point of view came fully up to what I'd heard and read about it. My intention to dig over more garden space before hard frosts came had appealed to me as an easy task over which I need not rush, so as to enjoy the fine spell. But just as I'd begun, Herb Morton called to say he'd been thinking. His water supply, being close to the surface by mere percolation down the slope, sometimes froze up in winter. His cows poached the boggy places in summer, and would I take the job on of laying a pipe from the spring head near to where mine was placed? Judging by what he'd seen I could get the job done in a couple of weeks he said. With some feeling of obligation, and for the sake of neighbourliness I could but agree, even though I'd had a bellyful of that kind of digging.

I began at the top, in the quagmire made by the emerging springs, by making another catch pit, into the solid clay below. The meadow was unlevel, and before long I found that, in keeping down to the regulation three and a half feet depth, there were banks to cut through to maintain an even fall for the pipe, which brought me so deep that I could barely see over the grass turf. But for that it was fairly even digging, with only patches of clay and seams of gravel and not so many rocks. Rocks were the farmers' curse around these parts. They were mostly rounded reddish granite boulders, of all sizes, and arable fields had not only piles here and there against fences and hedges, but often in the middle as well. Some were only as large as footballs, others must have weighed a ton or more. Herb Morton had spent a day with tractor, chain and levers, hauling out a dozen or so I'd located and uncovered, in my meadow which he ploughed after the storm, and when at last they were rolled out, he hauled them to the nearest hedge on a 'stone boat' sledge built for the job.

It took ten days to dig Herb's trench, by the time I was close to his barn, with only twenty yards to go. For company, a fat hog would sometimes come snuffling round, and I never thought to ask why the animal was allowed to roam on its own in the meadow. Coming back to work from lunch one day, I saw Herb standing over my trench, poking something below with a pitch form. "The durned thing," he said, "with all the feed there is, it had to find your trench where you left off this morning, and now it's in and it can't turn round. I guess we'll have to drive it all the way up to the spring." The hog being large and fat was inclined to get stuck here and there, for my trench was only wide enough for me to work in. But by many a prod, foot by foot it gained the far end, a hundred and twenty yards up the slope at the spring and emerged snorting and frisky. "You wait — you b — —", growled Herb as we drove it down his approach road back to the farm.

On the way down he asked me what my plans were for winter work. I told him I'd been on the look out for a job though not of the type I'd undertaken a week or two before, when Oscar MacGill came to offer me a day's work. Being in need of the money I accepted, and he drove me back to his house where he lived as a bachelor of means. He showed me a building on brick piers; and in the three or four feet of space beneath his fowls had lived for so long, that their droppings had filled most of it, and would I get it out? Not wishing to be called 'jibber', I began right away, and finally emerged that evening having hauled out one way and another several tons of the stuff. Near the open ends it could be barrowed, but farther in, mostly on hands and knees, I piled it up on a sledge and dragged it out with a rope and tipped up the sledge well clear of the building. Oscar brought me two bottles of beer during the day, and it was in truth thirsty, smelly, hot and back-aching work. And at the end of the day, Oscar gave me five dollars which, he said was at the general rate of sixty cents an hour for farm labourers, plus twenty cents as bonus, since it had taken eight hours.

Herb Morton told me that some farmers went to work in factories during winter. Others did little but tend livestock or cut firewood, but there were two local jobs he'd heard of that I could apply for if I wished. The first was to help the man who had the contract for erecting snow fences along two of the Rural Routes including ours, RR1, which was two miles long. The pay was eighty cents an hour, and I told Herb I'd certainly put in for this, though it would only last a week or two. The other job was a one-man affair, and though only part-time, the Council on which he served had, on Herb's recommendation, specifically asked him to offer it to me, since others too, had considered me qualified for it. It was to become the district grave digger, at the cemetery centred on Millbrook. There were times, Herb explained, when frost prevented graves from being dug, and I'd be quite busy for a few days when a thaw came because the coffins at such times were in store in an adjacent vault in the cemetery.

Such offers tended to make me have the same kind of thoughts as did the Prodigal Son when forced to work in a far country. At least I, too, had a conscience and stark reality in conflict with pride and determination not yet spent. With Herb's water supply completed a few days later, I was earning money helping to erect snow fences and making enquiries still in hopes of finding more than casual work. I spent the Saturday following the offer of the grave digging post with some of Herb's friends and colleagues, splitting firewood for the church heating system, and it was then that I finally turned it down, with the thought that it at least was some compliment to my delving ability. Winter came down with sudden ferocity, and the cow was now in one of the stalls beneath the barn floor, on which hay and straw was kept. She was still lonely, still inclined to blare spasmodically, and now she was cold as well. Her milk yield had fallen to four or five pints a day, and she was not after all, in calf, which meant that before long, she would be redundant as a house cow. For the winter, I rigged up a frame work and put over and around her walls and roof of thick straw, with a canvas flap at her rear to give access for milking and one at the front for feed and drink. I split firewood and piled it to keep dry inside the summer kitchen and dug out a large voracious Locust (Acacia) tree by the roots which were the toughest of any tree I'd encountered and sawed this too for firewood.

*   *

December came and one lunch time Herb 'phoned me to ask if I'd lend him a hand that afternoon if I was not too busy. When I reached his house, Leslie Pritchard was with him, and we were shown Herb's new central heating system which just then was on full blast to see how hot the house would get. "Better not get too cosy," Herb said after watching the thermometer for half an hour as it climbed to eighty. I asked what the job was, for there seemed to be no hurry, whatever it was. Both men grinned — "You'll see," said Leslie as we made for the door at last. Outside there was a little cloud of steam coming from behind an outhouse. Herb went aside into his summer kitchen and came out with a little cloth bundle which he unwrapped to reveal four or five knives of different design, and then for me the penny dropped.

Herb said it would need the three of us to drive the hog over from the barn and began to warn me that my job would be to hold his back legs out as he was noosed and hauled up over a bar, ready for knifing. "And for God's sake — if you've never done this before — hold on tight. Don't let go or you might get slashed like I did the first time, ripped my wrist that old bastard did, and I've still got the scar." It wasn't so much the fear of getting hurt that made my stomach turn and revolt. More than once, as a small boy, I'd seen pigs being stuck this way, strung up, and child like had been transfixed by the appalling sight of gushing blood followed by the plunge of the still kicking carcass into boiling water. Now I was cornered. I'd been able to make myself perform several distasteful jobs since coming to Canada, and the thought of jibbing now stabbed at my pride, despite the horror I knew would come, and probably overwhelm me at the crucial moment. If that happened

I'd never live it down even if my lapse caused no harm. Such a risk was too great to ignore.

"What's the matter—you aren't yellow, are you?—now's your chance to get even with the hog that got in your trench a week or two since," Herb said. But I lamely said I couldn't go through with it, however sorry I was to let them down. Finally they gave up trying to persuade me; and Les said he'd have to go and fetch his seventy-five year old father living in Cavan village. I stayed with Herb, helping to carry firewood to his new heating store in the cellar, and before long Les returned. His wizened father stepped out briskly, almost gleefully brandishing a pair of knives he'd brought. "Where's that hog who's ready for me—cos I'm ready for it," he crowed. I walked across the meadow in a beeline for home, feeling a strange mixture of shame and relief, not looking back though I could almost see what was happening in my mind's eye.

Christmas mail began arriving. Letters from parents, relations and friends were especially welcome. One I did not expect was from Bill Moorcroft, the Diss Bank Manager, who had been a friend as well as a financial advisor. The contents of his letter were brief and to the point. He was not happy at the way things were going at Bressingham. He'd heard rumours and both his enquiries, and the state of my firm's account at the Bank backed them up. In short, if I didn't come back soon, there wouldn't be anything to come back to. Then two of the staff who had been reluctant to see me go, the farm foreman and Percy Piper, the gardener, wrote letters in which the indications there were too plain not to be ignored.

It took a week to reach a decision, even though this was more a case of needing time in which to swallow my pride. It was true that fortune had done anything but smile on my efforts to make good. But I'd made blunders, and I slowly realised that the greatest blunder of all was to imagine that six of us could live on what remittances I could expect from Bressingham, until I could establish myself with direct earnings. Boiled down, it was a mistake—or the foolhardy venture my father had said—ever to come to Canada; and on the personal and domestic side too, there had been more loss than gain. I'd failed and that was all there was to it.

On the financial side, we were scraping through, but only just and prospects here were grim enough for the future. The Island property had finally been sold in October—at a loss of $500 on the purchase price, but at least the Sissons had been paid off, and but for the home equipment on hire purchase, I had no debts. Even these could easily be paid off from the sale of furniture, if as I expected, the farm would not find a buyer till spring. There was no doubt on the children's part. They had had enough of Canada, even though now they were enjoying tobogganing for the first time, and having all the sliding and skating they could wish for. Winter over here was not, as I expected, a case of frost and snow staying for months once it came, but of violent changes. Heavy snow would be followed by frosts of forty degrees or more for a week or two, and then a rapid thaw would come. The temperature would soar by as much as sixty degrees in twenty-four hours, and fall just as rapidly a few days later. It was I decided, a harsh climate, and no wonder so few people bothered about decorative gardening. No wonder too, that these sloping arable fields were eroded, with some in the district already abandoned by farmers.

Myrah's reaction to my decision was different to that of the children. I had expected that she would not wish to return to Bressingham as housekeeper, and I had no intention of trying to persuade her to do so. It became one of those questions when one side waits for the other to provide an answer, and when some indication came that she had nowhere else to go I hadn't the guts to say what I really felt. She had gone some way in filling a maternal need for my three, and Philippa had fitted in reasonably well with them, as part of a family. For a woman of her calibre, and the realism I thought she possessed, it was pathetic. And if I had not the heart for my own children's sake and for hers, to split up, I hoped she would see that her future did not lie under my roof.

With the decision to return made, there was much to do. I booked cabins on the *Franconia* from New York to sail on 26th February, and then set about selling up, all but personal effects. The furniture, much as I would liked to have had it shipped back, had to be sold, and quickly. I accepted Leslie Pritchard's offer, without argument, to buy the cow for little more than half what I paid for her four months ago, glad to see her go. During a thaw I returned most of the soil and clay back into the big useless well and advertised the electric appliances so recently installed on hire purchase, along with the furniture, but hoped to have the cooker sent on because it was far ahead in design of any British make.

Though busy and anxious, time dragged. Having decided, I wanted to get back quickly, I began feeling resentful at the mismanagement that must have occurred at Bressingham. I wanted to size up the task that would face me on my return. With only three weeks to go a telephone call came from the hire purchase firm to say that I had broken my contract, and they would be sending a bailiff. I argued that the sale of effects would easily clear the amount outstanding, but this was not acceptable. The law was on their side, and if I'd not fully read the hire purchase terms it was no concern of theirs. The man arrived next day, and said he had orders to stay put until he received the $450 outstanding. He was not unpleasant but he had his orders to carry out regardless of the embarrassment to us. There had been an enquiry from a hospital doctor in Peterborough for a fine carved antique chest of drawers. He'd been to see it and would think it over. With no other hope, I telephoned him and he came over again, offered $350 and I had to take it. A farmer down the road offered for the 'fridge about half what it cost — I had to take that too and after only twenty-four hours stay, the bailiff left us, with the required wad of dollars.

When at last the day came, I hired a lorry to take the bulkiest cases and baggage to Peterborough, with Myrah and the children going by train. We stayed at an hotel that night and left on a fast train next morning, changing at Toronto, and passing into U.S.A. after dark. There was another change at Buffalo, just before midnight, not to get on to another route, but because the heating system had gone haywire. The children had at last dozed off in spite of the heat, but having to wait an hour in the bitter cold for a relief train to turn up was miserable in the extreme.

New York next morning was of some interest, though I fell foul of a bunch of hotel porters in my ignorance, followed by cussedness, over the tips they thought inadequate. A sense of peace and quietness filtered into my mind once aboard the *Franconia*, and though there was anti-climax when fog-bound for forty-eight hours outside Liverpool, the seeds of a new and more realistic determination were beginning to take root.

For two weeks we were split up, as a family. The boys went to Sheringham to stay with my greatly relieved parents, whilst Myrah and Philippa stayed with hers in London. I stayed with Bill and Margaret Moorcroft in Diss, with the house at Bressingham being let off as two flats and two downstairs rooms, including my study, being used as offices for the business. As intended, I'd taken the management by surprise and spent the first few days prowling around and finding out why the place had gone back and who was responsible. The manager must have expected the dismissal I gave him for dereliction of duty, and general incompetence. Even "Bella", my old steam engine had been cut up for scrap, and this made me very angry indeed. I was the cat and he and one or two more were the pigeons, but it served no purpose now to rake up details of what I found as a result of those prowlings and questionings. It is enough to say that just as I'd been glad to shelve my responsibilities twenty months before, now I realised that in a sense, I had defected. And as a penance, if nothing else, was glad of the chance I scarcely deserved, to shoulder those responsibilities once more. I was glad too when the tenants in the house were able to move out and to make room for us to live where we belonged, and above all to realise that those of the staff I'd left behind who were still there, were glad to see me back. It was a shattering experience, and the more I realised what I had glibly let go, and so nearly lost, the greater and more imperative came the new challenge I could but accept with both hands.

Chapter Nine

IF EVER I needed both hands it was when I took over the reins at Bressingham, once more. In less than two years stocks of plants had dwindled to an unbelievable extent. The best selling kinds had been allowed, in many cases, to drop below the danger level — of insufficient left in reserve for propagation to make up for those sold in one season. The pot grown alpines were choked with weeds and for the first few days I acted as ganger to weed those not so bad as to warrant re-potting as the quickest way. The sterilising boiler was set to work again, and with a mixture of weed-free soil on the bench, I also set up the pace for potting. A few spring orders were still coming in, and to ensure good quality and packing, these I handled myself after tea each evening. The feel of soil and of the plants themselves was like a balm, as the first notions I'd had on my return of selling out and going to New Zealand faded in the realities of the task of rebuilding what tangible assets I had left.

Money was tight in the extreme, and the Bank insisted on a new valuation before an overdraft could be granted which would tide us over. Staff had dwindled to about twenty-five, which was inadequate for the work crying out to be done and a few more helpers were desperately needed, so as to have saleable stock by autumn. The first priority must be to make the land productive, whatever the crop, and to keep all other expenses, business or private subordinate to this. For the first time since 1939 I was handling soil at close quarters. Peat, sand and fertiliser had to be mixed in with sifted sterilised topsoil to make potting composts. The proportions of each needed variations according to differing types of plant. The truly alpine kinds, such as are native to high altitudes, required a more gritty mixture than those that grew at lower levels. All of them when potted had to be bedded in sand, as a medium to prevent them drying out or falling over. This 'plunging' of little pots was a skilled but rather monotonous task, but the resulting neat and orderly new beds were pleasing.

It was less pleasing for me to discover we had no suitable sand for the digging on the farm. Sand lay under many acres in or just above the fen level, but it was not sufficiently open and porous. Used for plunging it would not permit good drainage. One way and another drainage was a real problem. Good as it was, the natural soil containing a portion of fine sand particles became compacted or panned when wet. A footmark became a puddle if it rained following a tread over dampish soil, yet unlike most clay based land, did not pick up one one's boots, or stick to a spade. The plunge beds I laid out for alpines proved to be badly drained not only because we used our own dug sand, but because the soil on which the beds were laid was made tight and impervious by the feet of those who worked on them. This mattered little in summer when the beds had often to be watered in any case, but in winter such wetness could kill dormant plants unadapted for such conditions.

Pipe draining of all the upland was obviously a task I had not bargained for, and in between times, trenches two feet deep were dug from the worst of the low soggy places and drainpipes laid to the nearest ditch. This was not the systematic way of doing it. I knew well enough that to underdrain a field, levels should be taken and rows of drains a few yards apart should be laid but that would be time taking and expensive. Wet places showed up as drying spring winds came, to prove that the uneven subsoil was holding water close to the surface, but time and funds allowed only for the worst patches to be done. And it had to be done by hand digging, for although at that time mechanical trench diggers were coming into use, to hire one of these heavy machines just for wet patches would have been ruinous, not least to the soil itself.

As the summer advanced orders for autumn despatch were encouraging. It had been a less laborious summer for me than that of 1949 when I had so much heavy digging in Ontario, but the hours of work had been just as long and my mind almost as full of anxieties. But it had been more satisfying work and had included a fair amount of propagating, of handling small seedlings and taking cuttings which were inserted in sandframes to make root. This was work I liked, and part of the process was to train local helpers who were quite unfamiliar with such work. In September I decided to build a packing shed, as an additional bay to the shed I'd built in 1948. But in one corner of the site, when laying the concrete foundation walls I came across a wet patch and suspected a spring. A test hole revealed water at three feet, and this I thought could be utilised. The irrigation bore hole was some distance away and though it yielded abundant water, it would be cheaper and easier to use what little water was needed in the packing and potting shed if I were able to dig a well on the spot, just outside the new shed.

Using as always the top soil for potting, I found no subsoil even at three feet. It was black, sandy stuff, and when down to water level my feet began to sink into it. It was in fact quick sand, but the grey-black colour indicated that someone long ago had also dug there, either a well or a little pond. With the water coming in as I deepened the hole, four feet across, it brought in fine grained oozing sand, and the sides began to cave in. The old method of using bricks laid on a spokeless cartwheel was useless in this case, because running sand not only prevented a level drop under the weight of the bricks, but dislodged the bricks themselves almost as fast as I placed them in position.

The modern method for well casing was to use concrete rings and knowing I'd never get deeper than six feet in this treacherous subsoil, I procured only two, three feet by three feet across, and letting in the first one, strove to level it before digging again from inside so allowing it to sink as I dug. But this it would not do. Working within its cramped confines I hauled up bucket after bucket of soft muddy sand, only to find the concrete ring sank on one side but not the other. A piece of flint under that side had been enough, but having grovelled this out, it was then the other side which refused to drop. Under this I found the sole of an old boot. It had a square toe, and this dated it to be at least a hundred and twenty years old. I sweated in exasperation. Last year I'd dug far deeper wells with no sign of water and now, having ample water only a few feet down, was finding it nearly impossible to make a well, because of this running sand. Time and again my gum boots went down and when I succeeded in raising one foot the other sank in to be just as difficult to heave out. As I trod about, in only a few inches of water, the stuff beneath was alive with movement, and still the concrete ring refused to go down level so that the other could be fitted into it and complete the job. For most of two days, with one helper on top, I laboured there. In the end, with the first ring askew and its top not far below the surface, and with almost as much sandy mud inside, despite all I'd taken out, I had to admit defeat. I also had to leave the concrete ring where it was, for it would have taken a powerful crane to lift it out again, embedded as it was.

By the following spring my confidence was growing in the future both of the farm and the nursery. Stocks of plants had been doubled in one year, and the goodwill of the business was returning. The need for piped water in and around the nursery, as distinct from the portable irrigation, had become vital, and having bought some second hand piping Don Hubbard and I began digging trenches in which to lay it from the borehole. Using two inch diameter to begin with, we went down to about an inch and a half for the branches and an inch for the stand pipe, and with a second hand Fire Service pump, water was available where it was needed most. That summer we dug two feet deep trenches amounting to half a mile in total length, threading and jointing pipes as we went. Don, a local man who had come to work on being discharged from the Army in 1946, was an ideal mate for the job. He enjoyed the work, and when a pipe was fixed he'd wipe his brow and say with a grin, "I bet that'll never leak!"

If I knew just how much of my time over many years has been spent either in taking water to where it was wanted or to getting rid of it where it wasn't, no doubt I would be somewhat appalled. With the Bressingham farm divided into lowland and upland, the former was nearly always too wet and the latter, when moisture was most needed, was often too dry. Early in 1952 I tried to improve the drainage of two fen fields in two different ways. Both were potentially good nursery land. One, known as Poplar Field because I used part of it to grow young poplar trees for sale after failing with plants because of flooding, was of eight acres, and square in shape. Remembering that in Holland, and in parts of the fens, long narrow fields made for better drainage, I had a series of ditches dug. It more or less divided the field into six long narrow strips on the principle that the shorter the distance excess water has to go to find an outfall ditch, the quicker it would drain. Already in the six years since my predecessor first ploughed it up from marshy grass, it had been the scene of three crop failures. The first was of oats in 1946, the second of potatoes in 1948, and the third of a large number of nursery plants in 1951. Some of these we rescued. A January flood early in 1952 had subsided with a hard frost, and left a roof of 'cat's ice' over the dormant plants. It was then that I decided on dividing the field into strips. The ditches were dug by a hired excavator, six feet wide, and the spoil from these raised the level a little, even if the strips made for more difficult cultivation.

The other field, adjoining, was of seven acres. Across it obliquely ran a low sandbank, twenty to thirty yards wide. In between, the peaty strips were lower by a couple of feet, but this slight difference in level was enough to make a vast difference in the growth of plants. The peat, up to seven feet deep, quickly became soggy and rain water refused to soak down and away. In a dry time it would turn hard and lack of aeration stunted plant growth. But when dry, the sand banks produced poor growth because the soil dried out and was too hungry to sustain growth. So it was that a man with a tractor fitted with a rear scoop, scraped off the top soil from the sand bank and then dug out a foot or more of the soft yellow sand from below and spread it over the peaty low places. When that was done, the top soil was replaced, and the field ploughed, but the operation again proved only partially successful.

Soon afterwards, hundreds of tons of soil from road widening was dumped on a peaty area which through lack of sand had been left untouched. The curious thing about this operation was that by the time lorries and dumpers had spread about six inches of soil and subsoil over this area of about two acres, it was little if any higher in level than before. An additional six inches of soil should have raised it by that amount, but I realised that the weight of lorries running about had compressed the underlying peat. There was still more soil to come, so the process was repeated and several more inches depth was spread, but this presented a second problem, because no plough we had could penetrate deeply enough. The pan created in the peat had to be broken up again, and some of the original black soil had to be brought up so as to mix in with the raw roadside stuff. It took many ploughings and workings, as well as two years of fallow, before that two acres could be cropped again.

In the few slacker periods of winter or whenever extra rainfall came, I prowled round the fen fields with a spade, hoping to find some place where by throwing out mud or some obstruction, the excessive waterlogging could be relieved. On one field, for a trial, I asked the ploughman to make stetches. This meant that a few furrows were turned inwards, so that for a few yards in width, a strip would be slightly raised, leaving a double open furrow between one strip and the next, for quicker drainage. This piece was planted that autumn with thirty thousand young Christmas Roses (Helleborus Niger), but by spring, following a rainy spell, we were having to pull them out again. Water had stood almost covering the field, and when it left, the plants lay with roots exposed to the wind, and the soil panned down again to make losses certain if they were left to take care of themselves.

It was disheartening. I was convinced that plants would thrive on this sandy black soil, if only the water would let them. The winter water-table — the level at which it stood below ground — averaged under two feet in depth. In summer, the average was four and if by some miraculous means, these winter and summer levels could have been reversed it would have been ideal for plant growth. But it was not to be, and there was nothing I could do except to complain and appeal to the authority in which control of the river was vested. The thirty acres which had been reclaimed from waste in 1947 was sown down to grass in 1951 and 1952, other crops having failed in the years between. Grass grew very well and produced abundant hay and rich grazing. To graze it, cattle had to be bought and paid for. Fences had to be good and strong, lest they broke out and damage the dyke or banks, or become ditched. And with fencing to prevent this, cattle had to be provided with water troughs for drinking, which had to be kept filled. For hay making, fences mattered less, except that when cut and baled the sward greened up quickly again and needed feeding off until autumn. But on such low lying land, with each field bounded by shelter belts and often a dense wood of alders and willows on one side hay was difficult to dry out and make. It needed turning almost every day with moisture rising continually from beneath to keep in the dampness. June is the month of haymaking. For us it was the month of haycutting and if cut in the first week of June, it was not finally cleared from the field till well into July.

The low land of Bressingham was baffling and tantalising. I'd fondly believed, when buying the place, that with the experience I'd gained at Burwell, on a much larger area, it would be a piece of cake to reclaim the thirty or forty acres here. I also thought I knew all I needed to know about soil and its treatment, but though I had to admit by 1952 that this was far from being the case, it still intrigued me, and I refused to believe I was beaten. I still had one or two ideas germinating in my mind about how to master these problems, but they would have to wait until time and funds allowed them to be put into operation.

By way of relief, and to put ideas of a different kind into operation, I decided to dig up the large lawn in front of the house. There had been a tennis court there, but when we moved in October 1946, it had deteriorated into rough grass. To the north was a half moon shaped shelter belt of evergreens, and there were one or two fine oaks and sycamores at each end. With the needs of the nursery coming first, plus the neglect resulting from my Canadian venture, very little gardening had been done, beyond growing vegetables for the house, and our predecessors had shown little interest in ornamental aspects. But I was a nurseryman, specialising in hardy perennials, and though I'd given very little time or thought on growing them other than for sale, I decided that it was time to begin, having more scope on such a site as this.

The conventional herbaceous border was of a long narrow strip with some kind of backing—wall, fence or hedge, behind. Such borders were notoriously tedious to tend and maintain and they called for an inordinate amount of staking. Pondering over these faults and the reasons for them it occurred to me that given a more open position with maximum light and air for plants that needed it for good growth, beds should have all round access. The tallest kinds should be in the middle and with such access, maintenance would be much easier and the view much pleasanter.

I called them "Island Beds" and the half dozen beds I made in the old unkempt lawn were of rounded but irregular shape in keeping with the surroundings. All I had to do was to chop up the turf and then dig deeply. The soil, as could be expected from beneath old sward, was soft, rich and fibrous. It was medium—neither sticky nor sandy and I reckoned it was about ideal for plants. It was also a good thing to have reserve stocks for the nursery, to grow plants under natural conditions instead of, as in the nursery, having to grow them for one season only.

The more I followed up the notion of island beds the more rational and sensible it appeared, and I wondered why I'd not thought of it before. What began as a notion, had grown into a firm belief by the time these new beds were planted. By the following summer, belief had grown into conviction as even more evidence than I'd expected came in support of it. And with it came a budding ambition to carry the thing much farther, though this, too, would have to wait until time and funds allowed.

If luck over the past few years had often gone against my various endeavours, it was with me over the choice of 1955 for the next project in which earth and water were chiefly involved. Cleaning out and enlarging the horse pond in 1946/7 brought no profit, but it had brought pleasure. Having had access until coming to Bressingham to water as a means of pleasure, whether for skating, fishing or any relaxation that water can provide, the pond was some mitigation. But it was too small, being only about forty yards across its roughly circular shape. On a bank to the east, raised by spoil from the pond, I'd planted a score of Scots pines. By now, those that had escaped being cut off when the grass was mown were tall enough to be seen and avoided in future but two weeping willows had grown twenty feet high. A wide shallow ditch had been dug by the dragline in 1946 to provide some spoil with which to raise the bank low side of the pond so as to keep a higher level of water, which otherwise would have spilled over into the adjoining fen field. But this ditch was only fifty or sixty yards long, giving the whole the shape of a frying pan with the ditch as its handle.

There were two or three reasons and excuses for making the pond larger. Had I been motivated solely by profit, these would have been nipped in the bud, but it was useful to have a fairly good excuse for the expense of making the pond into a small lake. If the cost was not counted, and if I'd been positive of the end result, it made sense to sacrifice an acre or two of land in one field in order to make eight acres in the field adjoining fully productive. This was the Poplar Field, with its intersecting ditches which had not proved very effective in improving the drainage, because of the choked up river. But to add the spoil of soil, sand and clay from an acre, dug several feet deep, should improve the quality of the peaty soil as well as raise the level. Peat lacks mineral matter. Sand and clay were mineral and I could tell myself or anyone else quite convincingly, that this project would be worth while.

We began in July 1955, by peeling off the top soil from beyond the end of the pan handle ditch. I'd marked out the area with sticks, pear shaped, with the bulge at the far end, with the idea that this would be the deepest and loaded tractors could climb the slope easily, run into the adjoining Poplar Field, dump loads and come back for more. The top soil was kept to raise the bank on the north, or cultivated side, so that when filled with water this would be well above danger level. Being almost at the bottom of the gently sloping side of the valley, the bank on the low side had to be raised much more, but it would only be guessing to gauge what the water level would be when finally it was allowed to fill up.

My plan was to dig down as deeply as time and conditions allowed, and this was the reason for making a deep hole at the far end for it would act as a sump, draining the rest as the work proceeded. A smooth mud free digging surface was very necessary for tractors having rear scoops with which to pare off the subsoil and take away two or three hundred weight at a time. A proper excavator, feeding lorries or dumpers would have been much quicker, but to use one's own equipment and labour was very much cheaper. Robert and Adrian, now fourteen and fifteen, enjoyed being tractor drivers. It was summer holidays for them, and the job appealed since both were taken with the idea of having a little lake.

Below the top soil was soft sand, as usual. This varied in depth from two to four feet and below that was flinty clay. In the end where the sump hole was dug, there was a peaty pocket, in which broken antlers and half a rotted tree roots were found. Fresh water shells abounded, but no bog oaks came to light. At about seven feet down, the peat gave way to blue buttery clay, but the layer was only a foot thick, and below it was the 'bear's muck' type of peat. Ken Long was the star tractor driver, as the sump hole, about twenty yards across was slowly deepened. The sloping side grew steeper with increasing depth, and it became increasingly difficult to pull out after backing down and scooping up a load of heavy clay. With such a weight the front of the tractor rose up, and the rear wheels skidded, but Ken hit on the knack of encouraging the front wheels to rear up so that turning on its own pivot the tractor would swing its airborne front into the hole, to turn about, and this made the rear tyres grip so as to back out of the hole with a load quite easily.

For five weeks, mainly dry warm weather persisted. It was the first harvest for which our own binder was discarded in favour of a hired combine, and this made it possible to keep our two tractors at work on most days. At the end of the five weeks, about four thousand cubic yards of soil, sand and clay had been taken out and dumped in little heaps on the adjoining Poplar Field. The new pond area, about twenty yards or so wide, and nearly a hundred yards long, varying in depth from ten to three feet from east to west, was at last ready to be filled. The western end was left as a narrow dam against the pan handle end of the existing pond, and the great moment came to break through and let in the water. This called for care, for I was not at all sure of my levels and a rush of water might damage the newly-made banks. It took three days to fill up the new pond, but all was well.

Satisfying though it was to have this extra acre of water, of a shape that would take off any appearance of artificiality, the benefit to the Poplar Field was slow to materialise. It took several ploughings and scufflings to mix the spoil we'd spread over the surface, in with the peaty soil. The clay in general was not the bluish stuff which I knew was best for improving such land, but sticky boulder clay, and though it added mineral content in some degree, the level was not appreciably raised. This was the real bugbear. Soil structure was so easily harmed through excessive wet and a high water table in winter. The river lower down was in a constant process of silting up, nullifying our efforts, both to drain these fields and to build up fertility. The valley was bottle shaped, and the neck of the bottle was being squeezed in because it ran between high banks of sand. Deepening the river by excavator sent in by the River Authority in 1947 made no lasting improvement, for the weight of the sandy mud taken from the bed of the watercourse added to the pressure from the unstable banks.

Water weeds quickly took hold in the river bed, and after a year or so prevented scouring from the flow of water, because their roots held fast and their stems and leaves collected any drift of silt or mud. These were stark facts and yet I couldn't quite swallow them. Drainage would always be a problem, and flood or waterlogging always a potential danger, liable to incur losses at almost any time of the year. I'd given up annual cropping of about thirty of these fen acres and put the fields down to grass, but about twenty more lay so handy as nursery fields and were so potentially fertile, that I could not bear to give up the struggle on these as well. Thoughts of installing a pump capable of keeping excess water from them occurred more than once. But time and again they had to be dismissed, because to pump into a main water course would also involve banks high enough to prevent water from spilling over or finding its way back by roundabout ways. Every ditch leading into it would need sluice gates as well, and when danger came from heavy rainfall, constant patrolling as well as pumping would be necessary.

Nursery stock is far more valuable, acre for acre, than any farm crop. Losses through waterlogging and flooding would likewise be far heavier, but if I persisted in trying to utilise these fields for growing plants, chances had to be taken whilst doing all in my power to improve both the drainage and the soil itself. This was deficient in phosphates and potash. In places it was also deficient in such trace elements as manganese and it was remarkable how the latter showed up in certain crops. Potatoes were one of these and when they came into leaf, a yellowing quickly took place here and there. Test holes revealed that beneath these patches were an extra depth of peat in which shell marl had formed. In ages past there were hollows into which millions of various fresh water snails had drifted as floods receded and their shells in becoming compressed and congealed form a limey marl in which other mineral substances

(xxxii)   Aerial view of Bressingham from 800 feet taken in 1969.

(xxxiii)   The first island beds at Bressingham.

(xxxiv)   The gardens at Bressingham.

(xxxv)   Raised bed for alpines in Bressingham Gardens.

Michael Warren

(xxxvi) 'Bella' at work in 1947—the
Author's introduction to steam.

(xxxvii) 'Black Prince' before restoration.  *A. Beaumont*

(xxxviii)　The traction engines in 1963-64. 'Black Prince' restored seen on the right.

(xxxix)　Ready for opening time at the Steam Museum.

(xl) 'Gwynedd' on the 2 foot gauge Nursery Line.

(xli) The Waveney Valley 15 inch Line.

xlii) The restored 'Royal Scot' hauling the 'Duchess of Sutherland' before restoration, 1973.

S. A. Fenn

(xliii) Where the 2 foot gauge and the 15 inch gauge cross at the rear of the Museum.

(xliv) Interior of the steam museum in 1969 soon after it was built.   *East Anglian Daily Times*

present in ordinary soil, were absent.

I still believed the addition of subsoil from the new pond extension, plus liberal dressings of potash and phosphate, must be beneficial, even if the problems of drainage and soil structure remained. The temptation to give up trying to grow nursery plants on these low fields was outweighed by my own stubborness, and in spite of warnings and forebodings which were there to be seen, I chose to persist. The pond project was incomplete, and a lot more mineral subsoil lay there waiting to be taken out and used. It was now shaped more like a dumb-bell, with its narrow middle, and the next year, in spite of inclement weather, this was widened, though not greatly deepened, to make a more pleasing shape, and to add more sand to low places in the adjoining field. For this operation, a stronger dam had to be made at each end but one was not strong enough and burst before the job was finished. It was not completed until 1959, when with the luck of another dry spell the oldest part of the pond was greatly deepened and the spoil spread to cover a further three acres. What I'd taken over as a small horse pond in 1946, had thus, after much toil and sweat become a two acre lake — an amenity so pleasing that the toil could be forgotten along with the original reason for making it. It was not long before it appeared to have been there for centuries.

During the 1950's the insidious silting up of the river bed was relentlessly cancelling out every effort made to improve drainage and cropping of the fen fields. Appeals to the Ministry had so far met with no response and losses were mounting. Twelve acres of potatoes had been planted in 1958 on a field named Dye's Gap, with ample fertiliser to make up for deficiencies. It had proved to be a wet summer and autumn and with waterlogging, the crop was so poor that very little more than the weight of seed put in came out as a crop. Then hopes suddenly rose with the news that the Ministry had at last given the go ahead to the River Board to carry out a plan they'd prepared for deepening and widening the river. By early 1959 water levels dropped by nearly three feet and I decided to plant potatoes again on Dye's Gap, believing that much of the fertiliser we'd scattered the year before would still be available. More, was of course added at planting time. But as if to prove my impotence to master this land, the drought which enabled us to finish the pond digging dried out the peaty based Dye's Gap to such an extent that less than half a crop — only about four tons per acre of potatoes was harvested. I already knew that as a growing medium dry peat was sterile, just as I'd proved the harmfulness of water saturation. With ordinary soil, reserves of moisture are drawn up in a dry time by capillary action, but peat did not behave that way and if the contrast between 1958 and 1959, between too much and too little moisture had been sharp, it gave abundant proof that the balance was a delicate one. The happy medium, of enough but not too much moisture, was likely to be even more elusive than I'd imagined. Future efforts to keep water under control would always be in jeopardy.

The best land for nursery work had proved year after year to be the strip of sandy loam just above fen level. It did not quickly dry out, it was easy to cultivate and it was fertile. Plants were not difficult to dig out, nor did they carry much soil in the roots — soil we did not wish to part with, much less to pay carriage on as they left the nursery by rail to fill orders. Had there been more of such land on the farm I would have made use of it for plants instead of struggling with the ill-drained, unreliable fen fields. Now that the business had been restored, the extreme caution on capital expenditure could be relaxed somewhat and I searched the neighbourhood for some sandy loam that might be bought.

A further eighty acres adjoining came on the market, and this was bought between 1956 and 1959. Only a little was the type I most wanted, but some had been hired meantime to assist in the expanding acreage of nursery needs. One field was just inside Suffolk, beyond the old Waveney, from our Roydon fen land, but to reach it men and materials had to travel two and a half miles by road. Another field, the owner was willing to let provided we cleared the old blackcurrant bushes with which it was planted. This was even further away, and though it was cleared and planted mainly with phlox, the results were too poor to consider this as a long term solution.

There were times, during the fifties, when the need for a wider coverage of irrigation on the upland fields was desperate. With careful use overhead irrigation could be the salvation of newly planted nursery stock. East Anglian spring weather is sometimes vicious, with cold but parching east winds, day after day, week after week. Little plants, set in quite damp conditions during February or early March could be withering and dying for lack of moisture by April. Having once begun to make new roots, they could withstand such harsh weather, for the upland soils held moisture reserves on which to survive and grow. But it was moisture in the top three inches that set them growing and if this was lacking for long, losses could be severe.

The 1947 borehole had been a godsend, but it was sited too far away from the upland fields we were now planting, some of which were above the main road. This formed a barrier against any extension of the existing irrigation system at that time, and in that direction, so I decided to sink a new borehole, and chose a central position just above the main road. I reckoned it was fifteen feet higher in contour than the 1947 borehole, and if the water in the chalk was at a similar level, its rest level from which to pump should be less than twenty feet below surface. To assist the lift, we dug a square hole, twelve feet by twelve feet and eight feet deep, intending to place the pump in the bottom of this.

The derrick arrived and boring began. Our hole was already well into the boulder clay, but it was hard to penetrate. After five days drilling, it was only eighty feet deep, but I reckoned that within another ten feet, the chalk bed would be hit and then it would be easier. But it was still clay at a hundred feet, and as length after length of expensive tubing was rammed down, I began to worry. Hopes sank as did the drilling blade with still no sign of chalk. The surface of the chalk was not, as I'd imagined, level like a table top, with its overlay of glacial drifted clay. And it proved, we'd unluckily hit a clay filled hollow in the chalk, for it was not until the borehole was just over two hundred feet deep, that chalk came up.

The next hundred feet into the chalk was easy going, and by the end of the third week, I decided nothing could be gained by going any deeper. The contractor said he'd known cases where the layer of chalk had been cut right through, and the water instead of rising, had fallen as a result. The onus was mine since no one knew how thick the chalk bed was. To pump it clear was difficult. The milky water had come to within fifty feet of surface, but a surface pump could not bring it up to clear it and free the clogged up boring. Finally a submersible pump was fixed and after working for two days, the water cleared. As it cleared it rose in the borehole, but it remained, just out of reach of a surface pump which for our irrigation system was necessary. This would lift only twenty-eight feet, and the rest level in the borehole was thirty feet down.

It rained after a long dry spell, on the day that borehole was abandoned as a bad job. I had learned a little more, but it was knowledge dearly bought. I resolved that any other boreholes I decided to have drilled, would need to be on a lower contour. Soon afterwards a piece of very sandy land had become available. It had been a bramble and gorse covered waste, infested with rabbits and when enquiries were made, it appeared to be ownerless. It was known as Freezen Hills, which was a corruption of "Free Sand Hills" and probably never had a title of ownership. Much of it was so unlevel and sandy, that I doubted if it was worth the cost of clearing and cultivating, but because it was nearby, abutting on to some low lying fen land I owned, the task began, and a clearance was made. When cleared, both this and some adjoining land I'd bought in 1959 would need irrigating and another borehole was called for.

With less than a week's work, the drilling operator had a borehole which, at a hundred and forty feet, yielded water gushing under its own pressure from the top of the pipe almost at surface level. Because it was running to waste it had to be sealed with a detachable plate to be removed only when the portable irrigation pump was used. Three years later, with more land half a mile to the west acquired, a third borehole was needed and again the site chosen was very near the valley bottom. This showed how variable was the geological pattern of the district. To begin with it was flinty clay and after fifty feet of this, the drill came to a deep layer of gravel and then more clay. The chalk was not hit until it was about a hundred and twenty feet deep, but having gone down to make the total a hundred and ninety feet, water came up with such a rush that no pumping to clear the fissures in the chalk was needed. Again it had to be capped and it was estimated that this six inch borehole would be capable of producing twenty thousand gallons of water per hour with a large enough pump.

It has been said that under much of East Anglia the chalk holds immense quantities of water. Perhaps experts on the subject know where it comes from, but there are many unsolved mysteries about subterranean streams. In this region of low rainfall, it is difficult to believe that all the water, under constant pressure as it is, could be the result of rain finding its way down into the chalk. It seems more likely that much of it has come from more distant parts where both rainfall and altitude are higher. This would account for the pressure. It is believed that the general slope of the chalk surface below the imprisoning clay, is towards the east and it may be that springs emerge here and there on the sea bed.

Springs are also found at the base of chalk hills or limestone hills. At Burwell, there was a constant flow of spring water from the chalk, which collected by a large stream running at the foot of the slope to be channelled into the man-made Burwell Lode. Little rivers, such as the Snail, Lark, Little Ouse, Thet, Wissey and Nar are also spring fed from the line of chalky uplands running north from Cambridge to

Kings Lynn on the eastern side of the Fens. What has puzzled me is that these streams all have a westward flow, and yet thirty miles to the east, the pressure of underground water released from the chalk is towards the east. Taking account of the height of land, it may be that whereas the west flowing springs of streams take the water from the upper layers of chalk, the boreholes to the east, in the Norfolk-Suffolk bulge, release streams from a much lower level, once the overlying clay is punctured. I've heard of boreholes further east still than Bressingham which give a rest level, twenty feet above surface.

Water resources have become a vital factor in Britain and will be more so as population increases along with the startling increase of water consumption per person, to say nothing of industrial requirements. It is said that less than ten per cent of the water which flows out to sea from rivers is used, or that over ninety per cent of the rain that falls on Britain is wasted. This cannot be disputed, but it is the cause of much concern for the landsmen and country dwellers of East Anglia that already the reserves in the chalk are being drawn away to supply the conurbations of people further south. Those of us who have to rely on water they find beneath their land are already having to pay for the privilege, at so much per thousand gallons used. If what we pay contributes to schemes to supply distant towns and industrial concerns with water from the same resources below our land, resulting in depletion to the extent of making our borehole water out of reach, then we shall have grounds for complaint. Whether such complaints would be heeded is open to doubt, for it seems that nowadays policies favour the town and industry at the expense of rural communities and agricultural land.

For farmers, and even more for horticulturists, water is a vital necessity. For such as I, having had a long struggle to be rid of excessive water, at more or less the same time as striving to make good use of it when rainfall was too scanty, I can but harbour certain forebodings regarding the future. I have been as it were standing in the middle of a seesaw for most of my life. Having done what I could to put pressure on one side or the other according to changing needs, I realise how puny my efforts have been, and how great are the forces quite beyond my control. But even with this realisation, I have enjoyed moments when what I have been able to do, for or against water, has met with some, if only partial or temporary success. I cannot think of water as an enemy. In one sense it could be compared with that other potent element—fire—a good servant but a bad master. But whichever way one thinks of water or reacts to it, it is an element it pays one to respect.

Chapter Ten

ALTHOUGH as a boy I had ambitions for a time to become a geologist my knowledge and experience never went far below the surface. What could be grown in the surface layer of soil became too absorbing. Delving holes, ditches, wells and ponds were diversions rather than deviations from my main interest as a cultivator, both agricultural and horticultural. Of the two, farming in my experience was far simpler and less complicated, less exacting than running a nursery. Horticulture can be infinitely diverse; and there are specialists who grow nothing but such widely different crops as orchids, fruit trees, alpines, chrysanthemums and a dozen more to say nothing of horticultural food crops. From the time I left school, my leanings were towards hardy perennials, from tiny alpine plants, to such tall subjects as delphiniums. From the first I was intrigued by the immense variety in existence and quite apart from having a wide range of saleable kinds, I was drawn to collecting any species with claims to garden worthiness.

In pre-war days, there were a dozen or more sizeable nurseries having hardy perennials as the speciality. During the three decades since then they gradually dwindled; and it became nothing to boast about to realise that my nursery was by far the largest of its type in Britain. Some firms dropped growing perennials because they were less profitable than other specialities. I might well have done likewise, but for my love of plants which must have been stronger than the urge for profit. Whilst making a reasonable living even if return on capital was pretty low, I was content, and in deciding to make a much larger garden, to collect a wide variety of plants, I reckoned it would be more rewarding than sticking closely to purely commercial aspects.

By 1957 the success of my experimental islands beds was beyond all doubt. By then too, I was married again, and I was in a much happier and more settled frame of mind. Flora gave me wholehearted encouragement in embarking on a new gardening project. Beyond the shelter belt in front of my house was a park like meadow of about seven acres. It was studded with several fine oak, elm and sycamore trees and was level but for a low hollow of about an acre which had always been known as the Dell, even if it was only six to eight feet deep with sloping banks. The nearest point from the existing garden in front of the house to the sunken Dell was about thirty yards, and I decided to make a sloping pathway down to it, because I wanted to convert the Dell into a garden as a first step. The main reason for this was because it offered scope for growing plants requiring shade and moisture, for which artificial conditions would otherwise have to be provided.

With the path eight feet wide, the necessary slope of the banks meant that a lot of soil and subsoil had to be taken out. Using tractor and scoop again, much of it went to accentuate the depth of the Dell itself at one end, raising banks which had been a rabbit warren in 1946. This excavating virtually cut the meadow in two, and so that cattle and horses could continue to graze both parts, I decided to make a bridge for them to pass over. Access to the Dell would be under the bridge, and, by fencing round the new intake, there would be none of the dangers that come from gates being left unfastened.

If the bridge had been built with old red bricks from some demolished house wall in the village, it would have been appropriate, for the Dell had been dug long ago for brick and making clay. On the Ordnance Survey map the meadow carried the name "brickyard" and later we found the footings of an old kiln. As it was, some old bricks were bought from further away, but there were not enough to build both the bridge and the retaining walls of the bank on either side. An expert bricklayer built the arch with these bricks, and having used them all, I asked him to carry on with flints for the parapet. The method he used for laying flint was probably traditional, but somehow the results were not very pleasing. Too much cement was showing, and it suddenly struck me that there ought to be a better way even if it took longer.

Flint is a strange substance. It is not a rock forming part of the earth's crust, and is only found in nodules. These are said to originate from silica formed from the skeletons of almost primeval marine creatures, which with shells formed the chalk masses of Eastern England. As a stone or metal, the nodules grow in the chalk, into oddly shaped pieces, and when broken will splinter to leave a glossy surface, mostly black but slightly opaque. The vast quantities of flint stones in the clays and gravels and on the beaches indicate glacial erosion, and by far the greater portion of stones found in East Anglian soils are flints. Flint knapping is the most ancient of British industries and from it weapons, tools and fire lighters have been made from time immemorial. Twenty miles west of Bressingham, between Thetford and Brandon, Grimes Graves, where flints were dug thousands of years ago, are still to be seen.

Since Roman times, flints have been used for buildings. Most churches and very many houses are built with it. Some fine examples of knapped flint decorative building are to be seen in places like Norwich; but almost invariably these show the smooth black surface, skilfully embedded in mortar. But not all flints are black; some are almost white inside and out, whilst others are of a warm orange buff shade, or slaty blue. Flints from gravel pits vary greatly in colour and it occurred to me that a quite colourful wall could be built, if one set about it with patience and careful selection and placing of stones varying in size and shape. To keep the joints between stones from spoiling the effect, I found that I had to treat it like jig-saw puzzle, placing and rejecting stones till one that made a good fit was found.

My first flint wall, the bridge parapet, was a case of feeling my way with materials I'd never used before, and having to develop a technique with practice, by trial and error. It was late autumn, and to finish it before winter I used the car headlights, with the resolve to build other walls in the new garden when longer days came again. For the rest of the winter there was plenty of other work to do, if plants were to be growing and flowering next year. The floor of the Dell was meadow grass like the rest of the eight acre park. Beds were marked out with sticks, shaped to blend in with the trees and contours, and spadeful at a time, these were dug. The soil, despite the fact of brick making clay, was soft and loamy. Two hundred years or so had built up the humus and overlying sand had worked its way down from the banks.

There was, to my regret, no signs of water of the kind that could be used in summer droughts. Because of this lack, I led piped water from the house borehole to the raised bank at the east end, and dug a couple of holes to make into storage tanks. From these an outlet pipe with a concealed top could provide a trickle of water in summer for irrigation, along a little stream and into a pool. The bed of both stream and pool had to be made of waterproof concrete, and any overflow to be used for irrigation. The underlying sub-soil was porous; for previous observation had shown that even in a very wet time, any sogginess did not persist for long.

Someone, years ago, had found problems in supplying water for the house. I'd already found two abandoned wells, one just in front and the other at the rear. Another, much larger and deeper, had been dug in the lowest part of the Dell, to the west, but though what water it held could only have been drawn by a hand pump in the house, this too had been abandoned. It was as a result, no doubt, that the house bore hole had been sunk to put an end to previous occupants' water problems; for the well in the Dell even in winter was never more than half full and could only have been from surface water soaking into the clay. The natural spring had always held a great fascination for me, but this was not a district in which they occurred.

For the next four years, about an acre a year was added to that first intake. By then cattle were excluded altogether and the bridge could be used by people walking east to west, over the heads of those moving north to south and vice versa. It was in fact, an ornamental feature, regardless of its original purpose. Walls were necessary as retainers where banks sloped too steeply, and every year I found myself building them with flints and enjoying the work as a relaxation. With visitors coming to see the garden in the late fifties, there was the need for a shelter; and, having finally decided on a site, I spent all the spare time I could in building a round hut with the most colourful flints I could find. These came entirely from gravel pits, and I found more variations in colour by obtaining them as "rejects" — too large aggregates from widely separated pits.

1957 to 1962 was the period not only of garden making, but of searching out uncommon plants. This involved trips both in Britain and on the Continent from Sweden to Italy, and we always came back with the boot of the car heavily laden with selected interesting rocks and stones. The whole project was very exciting. The garden grew in size and variety, as new beds were dug, and filled with new acquisitions of plants, nearly all on a swopping basis. One of the last intakes was of level sandier loam, but because it lay next to the unlevel Dell, I decided to undulate this also to be in keeping. It proved to be a bigger task than I'd thought possible, but it was by no means the first time I'd visualised the end result of a project without taking sufficient account of the task in between. Where a portion had to be lowered in level, the top soil had to be placed to one side. Subsoil then had to be taken out and spread on the place selected for extra height. But first the topsoil from this too, had to be moved aside so that subsoil was added to subsoil before topsoil could be replaced on both hollow and bank.

The eastern end of the new garden was the last to be tackled. Still filled with enthusiasm, having already gone far beyond my first intentions and earlier ambitions as a project, there was only a couple of acres of meadow left untouched. To complete the job, to go the whole hog and take in the lot, seemed worth the extra effort. I wasn't in the least tired of digging out new beds, finding plants to fill them, building walls and generally expanding. All were island beds and it seemed a worthy cause not only to demonstrate on a large scale how well plants succeeded in them, but to have as complete a collection as possible of all worth while hardy plants, as subjects deserving greater appreciation by gardeners in general.

This eastern end was more level. To have taken in the last two acres without a break offended my sense of fitness and to create a break, I began another wall, fifty yards long, four or five feet high to hold in a bank at the rear and a sunken bed for moisture-loving plants in front. Beyond it, as the final intake, I believed a large pool would form a pleasing centre piece, with informal beds all round. This would be the limit. Six acres or more of garden, even if broad grass paths were left between the beds, would be enough to keep me going for the rest of my life, and interest others as well.

That was what I felt towards the end of 1962, when building the flint wall. It was cold work. Such building was not like digging for keeping up one's own body heat — both flints and cement were cold to the fingers. Frosty nights came and coverings of new work had to be made with sacks and straw. The final capping, with flat stones of various shapes and sizes was finished just as the year ended, and within a week or two winter began in earnest. For weeks on end, the surface of the soil, lacking snow cover, was like concrete. Water pipes froze up at two feet deep, and that was about the average depth to which the frost penetrated. It came as a grim and costly reminder for all would-be cultivators, that such elements as frost along with rain, drought and wind can come up with trump cards without warning and cause untold havoc.

The winter of 1962/3 caused me as a plantsman to revise somewhat my beliefs on which plants I grew were hardy and which were not. The absence of snow cover was the cause of the most widespread losses I'd ever known, but in monetary terms it was the business that suffered. For the first time ever, some of the staff had to be laid off for the duration because there was simply nothing for those with ability only in handling plants and using soil to do. Able bodied men could be put on hedging and ditching, but even the latter tasks, as manual work, had now become quite uneconomic with the advent of mechanical devices.

But for a few of us, there was a job to do, unaffected by frost, which had no connection with things that grow in soil. Since 1961 I'd been collecting old traction engines. The first one I bought purely as a personal hobby, as a relief from horticulture, a replacement at long last for "Bella" which had been cut up for scrap whilst I was away in Canada. During the summer, with the garden open for charitable causes, I'd noticed visitors peering under "Bertha's" covering tilt. This gave me the excuse I needed for putting a fire in her belly and raising steam so that both the visitors and I could savour the sight and smell of this old timer, built in 1909 by Burrells of Thetford, and to see her chugging gently about, giving rides to children sitting on the coal in the tender.

By 1963, there were about ten old engines in various states of repair or dilapidation. They were still cheap to buy, and most of mine had come from scrap yards — tractions, road rollers, ploughing and most dilapidated of all, an old showman's engine — "Black Prince". One or two had already been restored with the help of two or three voluntary helpers on winter evenings. With fresh shining paint and polished brass the result was very satisfying, especially on the day when one came to life once more. Because they evoked such an interest for visitors, and gave me such personal satisfaction as well, so began another project. It was a deviation this time, but without my realising it, it was to lead on to a programme involving earth moving and a different slant on soil and what lay beneath, even if the purpose was far removed from my basic job as a cultivator and plantsman.

Many of the enthusiasms which hit me during my life, petered out for lack of sustained interest. Looking back, I now see that some of them would have been far more profitable in pecuniary reward than others I have carried though just because they held my interest. Nearly all the hole digging fell into the latter category, and so did the steam engines. I made the excuse for collecting so many old hulks that they would prove a good investment. There would have been proof of this had I sold them again ten years later, but because I could not bear to part with them from Bressingham I gave them to a Trust to make sure they were never sold away. Before that my enthusiasm for steam had widened to include railway locomotives and by 1965 found that laying a track bed and sleepers for a 9½" gauge railway was a most enjoyable task.

This was another of those undertakings which at the time I believed would be limited in scope. To have a little engine I could drive, pulling truckloads of children on a track beside the garden had appeared as a final outcome, completely satisfying. But it wasn't. For the first time, I saw that by charging modest fares, steam engines could be self-supporting, and it only needed one season's running to set me hankering for another line, larger and longer, with trains to match. If visitors were willing to pay extra for a ride alongside the garden, which they could see on foot anyway, they would certainly be willing to pay for a longer ride in the nursery. This had to be barred to Sunday visitors. The fields were too scattered, and the temptation to pilfer would be too great for some to resist. But a ride behind a steam engine should be much more worth while; and off I went to Wales to see what was left in the slate quarries.

The half mile of track laid in 1966 was a rather haphazard project. I had little idea of how to set about it — about curvature and gradient limitations. There was only one place, beside the nursery office, for a station platform, and in the hundred and fifty yards down to the little lake there was a fall of several feet. The track had to wind through the pine trees I'd planted to follow the northern bank. It involved digging out in one place to make an embankment in another, and a brick and concrete culvert over the ditch that fed the pond. Curves were of necessity rather sharp, and in places the gradient was one in thirty. Alongside the lake it was level, and ex-B.R. sleepers sawn in half were about right to carry the two foot gauge track.

We now owned a Massey Ferguson tractor with a rear end hydraulic bucket for ditching, and a front end scoop. It was a machine that did as much ditching in a day with one operator, as a gang of four men could do in nearly a week. With this, much of the toil was eased and gravel in which to bed the sleepers did not have to be barrowed by hand. At the far end of the lake, another sharp curve or two, another steep gradient, and another culvert brought the track up the slope again. From there it ran back to the platform again, on the level, passing the beds covering three acres where several hundred thousand little pots of alpine plants were grown.

The half mile round trip took six weeks to lay, complete with rail. With two or three helpers, it had begun in mid-May and was completed by the end of June, and the first time "The Doll" was put in service, we ran into trouble. The eight ton engine spread the track before the afternoon was far gone, to such an extent that the passenger trucks it pulled became derailed on the curves. "The Doll" was heavy, and its long wheel base spread the track making the rails too wide for the wheels of the old quarryman's trucks I'd bought for taking passengers. A second engine, lighter in weight and shorter in wheelbase was hurriedly restored, and there were no more derailments.

The number of passengers that year warranted an extension for 1967. Leaving the pond side rail intact, points were inserted and another track was laid on to the valley bottom. The gradient had to be eased by a low embankment, and there was no avoiding one of the low peaty places as it crossed the field. The digger tractor made a ditch where it had to curve to take an easterly direction, and the spoil it yielded served for the track bed. The peat was six feet deep in places, and I had qualms. I also had qualms about taking up land and kept it as close to existing ditchs as I dare. These were deepened with the digger, and again the sand or peat that it threw on to the bank was used for the bed. In circling back up the slope, there were problems. The natural gradient, once above fen level, was about one in twelve — much too steep for a locomotive to climb with a load. The only way to overcome this was to ease it by making an embankment, beginning well down before leaving fen level. Sand lay beneath an unused patch not far away and again the digger tractor played a vital part. The pit it made proved useful as a depository for waste material from the nursery packing and potting shed.

But this new line held snags of another kind, when it came into use. The gradient back up the slope was eased to about one in thirty, but it was a bit much for an eighty-five year old engine to pull its train of five trucks carrying fifty or sixty people, on no more than a hundred pounds' pressure of steam. Sometimes, as driver, I had to stop and wait for pressure to build up before beginning the climb, and with the throttle well open it would gain the top, but trouble came when some passengers alighted back at the station to complain that sparks had burned holes in dresses and suits.

This was one reason for deciding to make a further extension in 1969. The bank was abandoned, and the curve leading to it was pulled out, to make for Freezen Hills field, where by adding another half mile to the route a more gradual ascent up the slope could be achieved. Another ditch to give good drainage and to provide a sandy peat mixture for the bed was dug across the low area known as Roydon Further Fen. This had been reclaimed a few years before, from an uneven low-lying sixteen acres which had in times past been dug for fuel turf. The old pits had been levelled off and bushes grubbed out, but it was so low that only summer grazing was possible as it often flooded in winter.

Having passed over this, I laid the track to curve through a grove of oak and birch trees, where soft sand lay only a few inches below surface. It rose gradually above fen level, and making the curve to the north for the return on the far side of Freezen Hills field, now part of the nursery, it was easy going, with the help of the digger tractor where excavations or embankments were needed. Sleeper laying was heavy work but I enjoyed doing it on my own. Using a straight edge board, sixteen feet long with a spirit level, I came to gauge the amount of gradient from the position of the bubble on the spirit level. Don and Arthur followed up with laying the rail, and being the flat bottomed kind, they fastened it with fish plates and dog spikes. I strove to keep well ahead just as they tried to catch me up. On some days, when the going was tough or difficult, involving barrowing or shovelling, I could lay no more than thirty or forty sleepers, but working in light sandy soil, with a longer day on the job, I topped the hundred once or twice.

When completed, this was a much more satisfying track for both driver and passengers to travel on. Speed was kept down to about eight miles per hour to avoid a rough ride, and to enable passengers to see more of the flowers planted where the line passed portions of the nursery. To see Freezen Hills as nursery was specially pleasing for me. Since the bushes had been grubbed out, it had shown practically no return. For several years after being sown to grass, the hay had not been worth cutting, nor had cattle been able to stay there long. It was the poorest of soils, with a high acidity and the sand content must have been eighty per cent in places, and it was uneven from the days when it was in fact "Free Sand hills". Belatedly, I decided to try a strip as nursery, and on this were planted such subjects as lupins and kniphofias ("red hot pokers") which could root deeply in a short time and preferred dry to wet soil. They flourished, and with irrigation so did other kinds which were tried the following year after which the whole seven acres came in as an integral and useful part of the nursery.

Each year, receipts from the railway increased. These went into my firm's accounts to offset both outlay and running expenses. They also encouraged me to lay another track, but by then much more exciting developments had begun. I learned that British Rail would consider allowing locomotives scheduled for preservation to go to private museums provided the accommodation and care was satisfactory.

The thought set me alight, and in the winter of 1968/69, the site for a large shed was prepared in which standard gauge as well as narrow gauge locomotives could be housed. This was a pre-requisite, and it was something of a gamble, for until it was built I could not be sure if my request to have BR locomotives on permanent loan would be granted.

The only possible site was on sloping ground just below what had been the stack yard for the farm, and just above fen level. It needed a vast amount of back filling to level off a slope of five feet in the hundred feet depth of the building. Subsoil was brought in, but with rainy weather it turned to doughy mud under the weight of the bulldozer that came to spread it. The footings were dug out, but it remained a quagmire all winter in which gum boots got stuck. Walls of concrete block finally rose to enclose an area of 12,500 square feet and with the asbestos roof laid, the surface within became firm at last. Three tracks were laid inside, merging into one outside at a gradient of one in forty-four, eased to this by a cutting through the parking meadow to make a run of two hundred yards on which to keep locomotives alive for visitors to see, hear and smell. Mobile cranes had to be used to hoist in the track. At one point, an old pit had to be crossed. At least it had been an old pit, dug for hoggin long before my time, but I'd had it filled in with rubbish including broken glass, pots and wire netting. Now this had to come out again to replace with loads of broken concrete.

The track bed, inside the shed and outside, had to be sound, for "Oliver Cromwell", the locomotive which took the "swan song" steam-hauled train on British Rail in August 1968, and came to Bressingham a few days later. Its weight was a hundred and forty-three tons, and three others, all between sixty and a hundred tons also arrived that year. It was the year of my railway mania, when steam fever took possession of me as the vision unfolded of making Bressingham the home of a sizeable live steam museum.

It was also the year in which excessive rainfall not only made for a very poor harvest on the farm, but caused immense losses to the nursery — at a time when our financial resources were stretched. The climax came on 15th September — a Sunday. Rain began at noon and only a handful of visitors came. I took a dozen insistent passengers round on the nursery line, but it was the only trip that day, for the rain fell heavier and heavier. It did not cease until next morning, and 4.38 inches was measured in our rain gauge. At the back of my mind I'd feared for years that such a fall would come again sooner or later.

Though East Anglia is generally a low rainfall area, with an average of 23½″ at Bressingham, now and then a little depression comes and causes havoc since outfalls to the sea are slow moving. Nothing so heavy as this had occurred since 1912, when over five inches fell on Norwich in twenty-four hours, and caused serious floods over the whole of East Anglia.

This one was more local, and we were about in the middle. By the Monday evening a hundred and fifty acres of our fen land was under water including sixteen acres of nursery plants in full growth. A start was to have been made, as usual in mid-September, on autumn orders, but many of those orders were never executed. The flood had come at the worst possible time for us. Because it was slow to recede, plants by the thousand were drowned being then in full growth. Had they been dormant, in a winter flood, they could have withstood it much better, but it was a blow we had to take; and none of the frantic efforts we made to get rid of the water were of any avail. The river, choked up again as it was by now, could not take it, and ten days passed before the land it served was showing black again, stinking with rotting plants.

It was the kind of calamity that might not occur for another fifty years and when winter came I decided to go ahead with the woodland railway as previously planned. This followed the course of an old ditch alongside the Causeway, filled up now with nursery rubbish and dumped subsoil. It was tree-lined and bushes as well as old stumps had to be cleared and burned, before a level bed could be made. The river had to be crossed and beyond, with a new ditch to provide spoil on which to lay the bed, we ran into trouble because of the water-logged peat. The Massey Ferguson digger tractor had to stand on mats or it would have sunk in. This hundred yard stretch was little better than a quaking bog, with water only a foot or two down in the black peat below. Sometimes the tractor slipped off its mat, but George the driver had learned a wrinkle or two and mostly was able to pull himself out by using the hydraulic digging arm, with a chain fixed to a tree. It was much too boggy to think of bringing in ballast, and it was a case of having to use what could be dug, even if peat was anything but ideal on which to lay sleepers. The stretch needed a new ditch anyway, for it was across the west end of the fourteen acre field we'd cleared of scrub in 1947, now panned down with wide puddles left by the flood, which had ruined what might have been a crop of wheat.

Frustrations due to waterlogging were offset somewhat by the act of clearing a track. Large trees were avoided, but great fires were built to consume the thickets of elder and dogwood. Once clear of the fen, on rising sandier soil, the track headed for a narrow wood of oaks, pines and wild rhododendrons. The latter, along with elders and briars, were so thick that it was possible only to cut our way through with axe and slasher. This was work after my own heart, and selfishly, I hacked out the ten foot wide track curving through the wood for two hundred yards more or less on my own, burning the bush and generally tidying up what had been for years a neglected amenity. Here and there, a little patch was dug in which to grow plants so as to enhance it, as a ride.

The task of laying sleepers had to wait. Those heaps of muddy peat would dry out in spring, and even if levelling the bed would have to be done by hand, it was along with sleeper laying, grading and curving, a job I could tackle with some relish when the time came. And the pleasure of being the first to take an engine over the completed track — another mile round trip — would be my prerogative as well.

This was in 1969. My railway mania was taking its toll in more ways than one, but it had not quite run its course. Another extension of the Nursery line was laid in 1970, making it a two mile run. It was made possible by the purchase of another fifty acres of land which included some more low fen which we did not need, but had to take, for by now it was only too clear that the all important drainage problem was unlikely ever to be solved.

This extra land lay to the east and south of Freezen Hills. Apart from fifteen acres of black fen some was good loamy soil on a southern slope, and the rest quite sandy — just right for nursery stock. One field of twelve acres was bounded by the river, but the middle of the field was boggy, simply because this, and not the course of the river, was the lowest part of the valley at this point. At this point also — known as the "Doit", where a north-south by-road crosses the river into Suffolk, the valley bottom was at its narrowest, the beginning of the bottle-neck. The peat strip was only about forty yards wide, against the half mile or so in width a mile to the west. This should have been the river bed, and probably was at one time, instead of being diverted through the rising sandy soil on the Suffolk side.

Having acquired this Doit field, we set to and made a new ditch straight through the peaty strip, splitting the field in two. An outlet pipe was thrust beneath the Doit byroad, and led into a similar ditch which our neighbour, from whom the land was purchased, continued. This Doit field had never been cropped, for some was too wet, and the rest too poor and dry, but having drained the low peaty strip, with its overlay of stiff alluvial clay, it grew a splendid crop of wheat in the first year. The rest of the field had to be fallowed to be rid of marestail and sorrel, but whereas no hard subsoil was found at six feet in the new ditch, sand and gravel was turned out by the plough only thirty yards to the south, half way across the fallow strip where the ground rose slightly towards the river.

Chapter Eleven

OVER the years, I have no doubt heaved several thousand tons of earth from one place to another by hand. Mostly, the effort as well as the result gave me some satisfaction. But now, looking back over those fifty years, I can think of ways in which the time it took would have brought far greater material reward, had it been spent with that kind of reward as the goal. What began as a boyish urge when time was of no account, to see what lay beneath the surface soil by digging holes, had never lost its element of curiosity. Later most of my delving was in order to obtain usable water, or to be rid of water which was causing harm. It is only in the past few years that garden and railway track making gave earth moving a fresh dimension.

Garden making, on the scale I undertook at Bressingham from 1957 to 1962, could come under the heading of "Landscaping", and one visitor dubbed me "Capability Bloom" having in mind the eighteenth century landscaper "Capability Brown". The latter worked for profit, but there was a tail end effort I undertook in 1963 which has not produced a ha'porth of profit so far. To the south of the garden, all that was left of the original home meadow was about three acres, sloping down to the Fen, above Dye's Gap. My sons Adrian and Robert had come home for good to enter the business and there was full family approval, for the idea of landscaping the lower end of this little meadow.

A bulldozer arrived, and in a couple of days scooped out a pond, twice the size of the one which took five men two weeks to dig by hand at Oakington in 1936. The spoil from this new pond—sand and soil—was spread out to form a low undulating bank in front of the untidy boundary hedge of Dye's Gap. Adrian planted a selection of trees, which in time would not only beautify, but form a shelter belt against the fierce south-westerly winds. The pond was filled with water diverted underground from a little stream running beside the lane leading to Dye's Gap, but left to itself the pond soon became thick with reed mace. Some day, perhaps soon, the margins of the pond will grow colourful moisture loving plants and choicer aquatics will take the place of reed mace. The trees, after a slow start, are now growing taller, and in between I may dig patches in the grass for special plants that like a little shade, though as it is, springtime is gay with daffodils. I may, or I may not live long enough to see in reality what was only in my imagination ten years ago, but as a piece of landscaping, it holds promise for the long term future, and Adrian has three young sons in the house he had built nor far away when he married in 1966. On his initiative an island bed garden of heathers and dwarf conifers was made as an adjunct to my own garden. Now that Robert and Adrian are running the farming and nursery business, as joint Managing Directors, I have more choice as to how I spend my time.

Robert is far more appreciative than I of the value of mechanical devices, as opposed to manual labour. But his generation and mine are poles apart in this connection, and one of the reasons for writing this book is to emphasise the vast changes that have taken place in my life time. Apart from large steam shovels and dredgers, there were no mechanical aids to earth moving when I was a boy. The bulldozer used for the last pond to be dug had not been conceived then, though tracklaying vehicles were given a boost by the 1914-18 war when the battle tank made its mark.

It is worth noting that two British firms who built steam traction engines for farm and haulage work were concerned with the development of tracklayers. It was Fosters of Lincoln who used caterpillar tracks on a steam engine for land work, which later played a big part in the development of the military tank. Fowlers of Leeds were the leading builders of steam ploughing engines. Amongst our engines at Bressingham is a pair of these, each weighing twenty-one tons. In their day — from 1890 to 1930 — there was nothing to touch them for ripping up heavy land, with plough, cultivator or mole drainer. Standing at opposite ends of a field, they winched the implement to and fro, edging along with each trip, and in the long hours their four or five man crews could plough twenty acres a day. Steam ploughs had their faults. The farmer had to provide coal and water, and he often grumbled to the ploughing contractor who owned the engines, of the state of the headlands and gateways which their great iron wheels had churned up. No doubt Fowlers believed a new German invention, on caterpillar tracks, would obviate such faults and reduce the number of crew men needed. This diesel engine machine, the Gyrotiller, came in about 1930 and Fowlers made these under licence instead of steamplough engines. They travelled over the land and left the soil stirred up deeply by rotavating tines. Farmers took to them at first, but later complained that they spoiled soil structure by stirring up subsoil and dislodging drain pipes, and in about ten years they too were becoming redundant in the face of competition from conventional ploughing and cultivating behind caterpillar or wheeled tractors.

Ransomes of Ipswich also built steam engines and farm machinery. They were first noted for horse drawn ploughs and most East Anglian farmers used them until after 1930, when it took one man and two or three horses to plough the usual day's stint of half an acre. With the coming of iron wheeled paraffin tractors, their two or three furrowed ploughs helped to oust the horse. This greatly increased soil turnover and cash crop acreage, because so much land had previously to be devoted to horse feed. An offshoot of the firm of Ransomes were pioneers in earth moving machinery, along with another similar firm, Rustons of Lincoln. This was the dragline, and for over thirty years it was supreme for digging drainage dykes, as well as gravel and other projects where earth moving was involved. A cab, housing a diesel engine and driver, revolved on a tracklaying bogey, and by pulling various levers, the jib, carrying a bucket fixed to a cable could be made to drop so that in pulling in, the bucket filled with spoil. When full the jib lifted it out to swing and empty the contents well clear of the excavation.

In the period of six years I farmed in Burwell Fen, the dragline caused the more or less complete changeover from manual to mechanical digging for drainage dykes. In my first three or four years, gangs of four men must have dug two or three miles of ditches by hand. But once the Drainage Authority sent down a Ruston Bucyrus dragline for a main dyke for which they were responsible, it was quite evident that with wages rising, the machine would be more economic in future. With one man as driver and another for shaving the sides of the dyke to the correct slope, it could dig three or four times as much in a day as could a gang of four men. The hire cost of the machine was little more than the wages of two men.

But still more progress has been made in the past twenty years and now old draglines stand about idle and derelict, just as steam engines did until the scrap merchants cut most of them up, before the enthusiasm for steam preservation began. The development of hydraulic power has brought another revolution to the practice of earth moving as well as to field cultivation and cropping. One sees these tractors, sometimes on tracks, but often on rubber tyres, which can be operated in an amazing variety of ways. They can dig and shovel, whether it be for ditches, trenches, pits or merely to scrape the surface. They are built in many sizes, and have interchangeable buckets according to the job required. Some can reach twenty feet outwards or downwards, and the big well I dug in Canada, which cost me three weeks hard labour, could have been dug by one of these in much less than three hours. One giant machine in County Durham opencast coalfield can move a hundred thousand tons of spoil in less than twenty-four hours.

There is no need to enlarge on the variety and scope of modern earth moving machinery. Some are monstrous, and a skilled operator with no more effort that it takes to play a piano, can accomplish with ruthless efficiency what it would have taken at least fifty men and several horses to do fifty years ago. So great a change in so short a time makes one wonder what developments the next fifty years will hold. Since machines began to provide power, with the invention of the steam engine, followed by electricity and internal combustion, mechanical inventions have proliferated in a tremendous upsurge. All have their origins in the spade work of the pioneers whose motive was generally to save labour or to widen and hasten what people could accomplish with manual skill and effort. Almost every aspect of industry became obsessed with progress through invention and the pace of development is continually accelerating. Yet human nature remains virtually unchanged.

The inventiveness of the human brain has in fact brought about a paradoxical situation. The movement towards labour saving for more people began in the Victorian era. The emergence of wage-earning people from drudgery and poverty had lagged somewhat behind invention, but in the past twenty-five years especially it has taken a great leap forward, and large organised groups of workers have gained such strength that they can almost dictate their own terms to their employers. Progress, as measured by the standard of living, has been hailed often enough as a worthy cause. Shorter working hours, less physical effort, more money to spend on luxurious inventions and man-made amusements is practically everyone's ambition, a goal worth striving for, and for some the be-all and end-all of human existence. For the majority of people, in most walks of life, work is now anything but a virtue and the rewards for work lies solely in the pay packet. Craftsmen, whose skill brought a satisfaction in a job well done, are being steadily squeezed out of existence by machines which produce more in less time. This is a generalisation and cannot include some sections of the community. but one of the best examples of the machine taking over is in agriculture; with a labour force of about a quarter of what it took to produce half as much, fifty years ago. Farm workers' wages, still low compared with some industries, have jumped since 1914, to nearly as much per hour as they were then paid for a week of fifty hours.

The paradox lies in the fact now emerging, that for all the progress towards richer standards of living, and so much more leisure, people seldom admit to being satisfied with the results, with things as they are. Probably more old people, who remember much harder times are satisfied enough, but they admit sadly that greater wealth and more leisure has not brought greater happiness especially to their succeeding generations. And this is largely true. Much wants more, and having gained it, yearns again for still more. It is one aspect of human nature, and it seems to be related to that which gives the spur to invention. Necessity is by no means the sole mother of invention. On the score of sheer necessity, it is far more necessary to invent a light beam to penetrate fog than to see and hear moving pictures by television. Television and the motor car are two outstanding examples of inventions that have proved to be mixed blessings, of inventions that emerged as luxuries and became rapidly to be regarded as necessities also by most people.

Happiness, like pain, is incapable of being measured, but there are plenty of signs indicating that the tremendous increase of leisure, of material wealth and the means of pleasure, has brought little if any increase in real happiness. One would have expected to see signs of more contentment, for more people, but this is scarcely the case, and it poses a question. Is there some unsuspected aspect of human nature which is being ignored in the mad rush to gain ever higher standards of living? Are we neglecting some basic human need, spurning what may be the antidote to the pleasant but maybe insidiously poisonous urge to grasp the apparent benefits of high civilisation, of technology, of less work and more leisure?

The switch from manual to machine made commodities has been dramatic but it has set up a vicious circle. Because machine minding is boring and monotonous, the worker loses interest in all but the pay packet and what to do with his leisure time. With both on the increase, more sophisticated machines are invented, to cancel out the rising costs of production, and this brings about a further increase in the worker's boredom. Boredom with work is a contagious disease amongst all those employed on repetitive tasks and can spread into shops, offices and homes as well, reducing any pleasure to the minimum to be found in work.

The process of mechanisation, and the increase of labour saving methods and devices is bound to continue. Its tendency is strongly accelerating and so is discontent and boredom amongst those most affected by it. And another growing tendency is for more people to do as little work as they can for as much as they are able to grasp by way of material reward. This is surely a symptom of a moral disease, (using both words in their true meaning), something which is creeping into our minds because we are overlooking a basic human need. This need, I believe, is to vitalise and fortify our minds and bodies as an antidote to the ill effects of the whirl of mechanical things of industrialisation.

Man as a species has evolved from the animal world because his brain as well as his physical skills developed, each complementing the other. Civilisation has, in one important sense, been the escape from a purely natural environment, an evolutionary progress from living in trees and caves and foraging for food. But in spite of the heights of civilisation mankind has reached, compared with primo-genus man, we are still animals, and our animal instincts as well as our basic physical needs remain with us. Because of this any attempt to make a complete break with the world of nature must have some detrimental effect upon us. We cannot be complete as positive beings if we try to live as if we were not part of the great complex of Nature with a capital 'N', and it needs no philosophic effort to realise that each one of us is subject to natural laws. Not does it need much reflection to realise that more and more people are being fragmented as individuals and torn away from the world of nature by urban life, industrialisation and the like, hamstrung by man's own inventiveness, as the general escape from living with nature continues.

Before the Industrial Revolution gained impetus, the vast majority of people were either craftsmen or landsmen. There were soldiers and sailors, shopkeepers and gentry, as well as parsons and professionals, such as teachers and lawyers, but in total they were still the minority. Whilst thinking mainly of men, women played their traditional supporting role to craftsmen and landsmen, but since they were also childbearers and home makers in most walks of life both men and women worked in a far more creative way than is the case nowadays. Poverty was accepted by many and skills were often inadequately rewarded, but it was the accepted pattern of life.

And those who used fingers and muscles as well as brains to good skilful advantage, in any trade or honest calling, would not starve, but would find a contentment in living which is so lacking in the modern world.

It is true that nowadays, more leisure gives opportunities for sports and pastimes for which both skill and energy are needed. This is good up to a point for those with skill and energy and time to spare, and even if competitive rather than creative, they are recreational pursuits which come as a balance or antidote to the stresses of modern life. Even so, sports and pastimes are often overdone and may become a waste of time, thought and effort, because they are not creative and should serve only the need for leisure. But there are vast numbers of people who do not go in for any form of recreation. They remain bored and unrefreshed and work is a burden to them. In some cases, through lack of urge, mental or physical laziness or simply that any kind of creative or competitive effort is too much like hard work, they drift discontentedly and often selfishly through life with no sense of purpose or fulfilment and none of the satisfaction that comes from "something attempted, something done". I believe that something attempted and followed through, even if it ends in failure or only partial success, as some of my ventures have, is better than jibbing for fear of failure or unwillingness to have a go. For any human endeavour incentive is the primary need. One needs incentive to accomplish anything in life, to attain the hall-mark of human as opposed to animal nature—what is above instinct or appetite—self preservation or sexual impulse included. Most people know this, though some may not be sufficiently aware of it, judging by the way in which they fritter away their lives and talents for the sake of what money will buy, all for lack of incentive.

A number of people are sufficiently aware of the need to create by taking up creative hobbies, such as pottery, painting and many kinds of handicraft. Occupational therapy for the disabled and mentally sick is a new and growing science, recognising as it does a basic human need, but it can scarcely work unless incentive too, is encouraged, as part of the treatment. The normal human animal needs outlets for energy to be used in conjunction with the brain, but if very little of either is required in whatever job or position we fill, then there is a vacuum. Into this vacuum, in far too many cases, can come the negative approach to life, the lazy attitude, the lack of incentive to use to some advantage the untapped, surplus brain power and physical energy. We become content to watch the telly for hours on end, or man-made amusements, pub conviviality, bridge or the like—harmless enough, often necessary sometimes for social reasons, but not to become the main or only way to spend ever increasing hours of leisure now available.

There are those who find recreation in quite helpful and commendable ways, such as various forms of nature study, music and the arts or as hobby collectors. There is virtually no limit in the choice open to those to whom recreation in these categories appeal, and there is considerable satisfaction to be gained from becoming an expert on a given subject. But unless some physical effort is also involved, for those with time and energy to spare, there is apt to be an imbalance, between the mental and the physical aspects, even if we are not fully aware of it.

Some people—probably a small minority, are aware of the need for physical conditioning as an antidote for harmful modern times. They may go in for keep-fit exercises, muscular sports, saunas, or the deeper more mystical practice of Yoga, and if such things help and satisfy the incentive to live fully and happily, more power to their elbow. I certainly have no grounds for criticism of them, nor for those that go in for such adult pastimes as golf, for those who feel the need for fresh air and exercise without becoming addicts, by allowing the game itself to dominate their leisure hours.

Of all the means of spending leisure time, gardening is to my mind, the one pursuit that can be the complete answer. I'm well aware that to some, gardening in any shape or form is anathema. They have neither the incentive nor the aptitude. They may say they can appreciate the beauty of a garden, but have not the slightest urge to cultivate or tend one themselves. Nevertheless for anyone, man or woman, who has a patch of garden, or the means of growing something, it stands as a door waiting to be opened into a hobby or recreation that can fill a very deep human need. If the means is no more than a window box or a place for a few house plants then it can scarcely be more than a mental relaxation. To reap to the full the benefits that gardening can bring it needs to be an outdoor plot, to be able to get back to nature sometimes by working physically and mentally in with nature. This includes digging, improving soil fertility and other operations in keeping with the rhythm of the changing seasons, and in season to sow seeds, taking cuttings, tranplant, tidy up and keep down weeds. In every one of these tasks there is a reward to be found, by those who approach them in the right frame of mind.

This frame of mind I would say, is to be fully aware of Nature and Mother Earth. Nature has its vagaries — evident in weather alone — and so have we, for as human animals, we too are part of the natural order of things. Like all living things, we too have our life cycle, but we are the only living creatures with a brain able to thwart or steal a march on nature occasionally, but also a mind capable of appreciating the beauty and wonder of the world of nature. A garden patch can then become our little domain within that world, subject still to most of its laws and rules, in which we are able to use our bodies and brains as evolved beings. Philosophers have said we become ourselves when we lose ourselves in worthy objectives outside ourselves. I believe this is nearer to the truth of the mystery of life and its purpose, than whoever said tha "being" is more vital than "doing". I, at any rate am not one of those capable of losing contact with externals. Living, to my way of thinking, is doing, using what strength or effort is needed, along with what skill lies in my hands, directed by what lies within my heart and head, to achieve or produce something worth while, if I can.

My working life began over fifty years ago, and I was fortunate indeed to become my own master, as far as work was concerned, when only twenty-four. Parental encouragement and circumstances as well as my own urges, made it inevitable that I should be a landsman in some way or other. Over that fifty years I've had to take knocks and learn lessons the hard way — often tackling uneconomic or impractical ventures in which effort and energy proved later to be largely wasted. Yet still the soil intrigues me, along with what it will or will not grow in response to my efforts. In this, I fancy, lies the secret of what it is about growing things which draws one in to lose oneself in the job. There is a recurring if not constant challenge which one almost automatically accepts, and every failure to cultivate something successfully, brings the challenge back — to try another method.

It follows that the greater variety one tries to grow, the more absorbing gardening becomes. Anyone who grows nothing but a few kinds of vegetables or flowers, cannot expect the same depth of joy or satisfaction as those who accept the wider challenge that variety brings. They can aim for perfection in what they produce and become specialists in even one kind of flower or vegetable. Specialising in this way often brings perfection, but once this is achieved, there is little left but to keep up the standard. They may enjoy the reputation that mostly comes to the expert specialist, be it potatoes or petunias, but in the process the important factor of self-awareness, of pride and conceit may well take first place because a challenge no longer exists.

True gardeners, who love plants for their own sakes, are at heart a humble people. They will admit to failures, but not to defeat. They are more aware of the wonderful world of plants in their infinite variety and are deeply conscious of how much more they have to learn, realising how little they know in comparison. They have an insatiable curiosity, by which increasing knowledge is obtained, and if they have any ambitions it would be not to become an expert, but to learn more about plants so as to grow the greatest possible variety as well as means and circumstances allow. Successes will generate a special kind of pride, because they are aware of all the factors, some of which, such as weather, were outside their personal control. Any sense of personal achievement comes into its true perspective, with the knowledge that complete success with every kind of plant they have is more than just elusive. And it is this that remains as a continuing challenge, and a spur sharp enough to prick any rising bubble of undue pride.

The secret of success, in whatever range of plants we grow, is to provide the conditions of soil and situation they most prefer. The more popular and therefore most widely grown kinds, such as roses, dahlias, and many others, whether annual or perennial, plants, bulbs or bushes, hardy or for indoors, have been so well written up by specialists and experts that one does not need to cultivate them on the basis of trial and error. By taking advice, one can be fairly sure of reasonable success. And because these popular kinds are mostly the most showy and colourful, growing them to as near perfection as possible may fill most people's needs. Any of these can be grown with no thought of becoming an expert, but simply as an outlet to one's appreciation of beauty, which includes the period of hopeful anticipation before flowering time comes. If it includes the tasks of preparation, of digging, planting and of maintenance, then this fills the basic need, like the bread to go with the butter.

For those with no garden plot, but with yearnings to grow something as a means of fulfilment of a deep seated need, I have only a few suggestions to offer. House plants are available in a much greater variety nowadays, and gas is less of a deterrent that it was in the days when only the aspidistras would survive. Climbers as well as foliage and flowering plants can be grown indoors in pots or troughs. Cacti are not very demanding either in space or attention, and the all important factor of variety is not lacking. Some people will have space outdoors for a glasshouse, though not enough for an outdoor garden. Some alpine plants in variety will grow in a cold glasshouse better than in the open, and in quite a small area the greater variety can be grown if small growing kinds are used — a role suitable for both cacti and alpines.

I was told of someone keen enough to grow fifty six kinds of tree orchids on one wall of the living room in a flat, and for anyone with a heated glasshouse, a vast range of plants can be grown including orchids. I also heard from a lady who filled her need for a garden by taking on two vacant allotments in which to satisfy her craving for variety, and to experience the full joy of cultivating the less common kinds of plants. Although the emphasis comes down on variety, I still believe that a sense of completeness comes to those who are willing and able to undertake the manual work gardening involves. In the open, especially, the closeness to nature is to be felt even in the elementary task of digging. It is not tedious if one strives to make it the craft it is, to lose oneself in the job as something worth doing well because it is the basic preparation for cultivating what one wishes to grow. It is also a seasonal task, and to be conscious that by turning over the soil before the onset of winter, adding richness maybe, nature will provide the rest — the weathering by frost, the nitrogen from snow and the beneficial working of worms and bacteria.

This direct co-operation with the elements of nature has been a vital part of human evolution. Skills have developed and the tools used in hand cultivation have improved over the centuries. Men began cultivating the soil probably over ten thousand years ago, and yet in less than one hundredth of that time, machines have been invented which make most people spurn manual labour as something to be avoided. In farming it had to be for sheer economic reasons, and farmers who persisted in the old ways simply went broke. This is not to condone those who tear up hedges to make vast prairie-like fields for the sake of the little extra returns in cash they do not really need, and probably spend uselessly and selfishly anyway. Mechanisation has spread into horticulture too, and though nurseries such as mine did not readily lend themselves to mechanisation, we now have of necessity machines for both planting and potting, as well as non-manual methods of keeping down weeds. Modern methods and techniques had to be applied for survival, but there is all the difference in the world between commercial horticultural production and gardening for pleasure and relaxation, into which labour saving devices of many kinds have been introduced in recent years.

Most amateur gardeners can work outdoors in keeping with the weather, as seasonal tasks come along. Garden plots are not often so spacious that their owners cannot cope with these tasks by taking advantage of favourable weather for each, which makes the job more pleasurable as well as effective. There's nothing like digging when its dry and cold to generate physical warmth and there's enormous satisfaction in hoeing when seedling weeds wilt within an hour under a warm sun or drying breeze. Whenever one is able to tackle elementary gardening tasks concerning soil cultivation, manual work is in my experience far more effective than any mechanical device. Mechanical diggers, hoers and cultivators are advertised to take the backache out of gardening chores, but in practice they are quite hard work to use on small areas. They will undoubtedly cover more ground in less time, but they are liable to spoil soil structure. Rotating blades in many types of soil, will create a hard pan below, leaving the top layer much too fine, and if such weeds as couch or ground elder are present, the effect is to chop them up into smaller pieces and spread them. Few gardens indeed would warrant the outlay of a machine for what should be preparative work of this kind, and few soils exist which are not harmed by its regular use as an alternative to seasonal deeper digging with fork or spade.

So much has been written and offered by way of labour saving devices that many people have fallen for sales propaganda, without realising that there are snags. This applies to chemical weed killers as well as to cultivating machines. It does not of course apply to such things as lawn mowers, edge and hedge trimmers, and others which are outside the actual work of cultivating and cropping the soil. It is mostly from experience that one learns to be selective in seeking mechanical aids. But if it can be accepted that certain tasks are best performed by hand, in conjunction with nature and that by so doing both body and soul are stimulated by the exercise, as skill and craft improve, a happy medium is reached which is bound to be satisfying and rewarding.

The soil is alive. It contains elements beyond our knowledge just as it contains far more living organisms and bacteria we cannot see, but even the worms we can see when digging have their place in the natural order of things which is such a vital factor in fertility. To find the ways and means which we can of improving that fertility is in itself a worthy cause. Some cultivators become almost rabid in this belief in organic cropping and whilst there is no doubt that, as a practice, the highest state of fertility is reached, there are many ways of improving fertility without making a fetish of it. Compost making, for example, is quite laborious, but it becomes worth while in the knowledge that waste is utilised to the best advantage. If what comes from the soil in some shape or form, can be returned to the soil in a form that will enrich it, the process is fully in keeping with nature and must be right.

It is in such matters that the mind needs to work as well as the body. The gardener who merely slogs, whether or not he enjoys the effort, can gain very little if he does not use his mind or brain as well. One needs to develop a full understanding of the task in hand not only to make the best job of it, but to know what end result he hopes to achieve. Hope and faith are essential in the mind's eye, and when working in with nature, one has to be crafty, and craftiness includes building up an understanding of the soil, its constituents, structure and behaviour under varying weather conditions. Skill comes with practice, and has a snowballing effect because in seeing the results it leads to greater skill and a craftiness which amounts to love as time and experience add up. In the process, manual work can change from being a tiresome chore to a challenge one gladly accepts in the knowledge that it is wholesome and good all the way. Whatever one chooses to produce from the soil — whether it be for the belly or for beauty, or merely curiosity, to find out from the infinite range of what can be grown is that which gives greatest satisfaction to the cultivator.

There are cultivators who have practiced good husbandry as a matter of course for a long time, who know in advance, barring accidents and Acts of God, that their efforts will meet with success. They know what the soil needs and make sure those needs are met in the right order. Such people are so much in tune with nature that it becomes second nature to them, and they have no need to ponder over the more scientific aspects of cultivation and cropping. They are, however, unlikely to venture into the realm of plants to grow for beauty's sake with any deep aesthetic appreciation, but in general they are rewarded with enviable contentment of mind. Such people are craftsmen, equal in stature to those whose work involves metals, wood, clay or paint, all of which had their origins in the earth.

The very rapid switch to mechanisation, has put less and less value on personal skill. So many workers cannot identify themselves with the product. This applies in many other spheres of modern life as well as in the producing industries, and this fact is only just beginning to emerge in thinking people's minds. It is surely a basic necessity of life to many, to be able to fall back on some task or some worth-while hobby which will act as a safety valve for the boring, frustrating kind of work they have to do in order to live.

Thinking back, I can see tasks I undertook which proved to be a waste of effort, as experience I had to gain, because of the temperament I grew up with. Some of those projects had no other inspiration than curiosity or just a hunch that it would be worth the effort, even if it soon proved otherwise. But when such a hunch developed, as first results spurred me on, it brought abundant reward, because something I was lacking within, was being satisfied. Without fully realising it, I was identifying myself with the job. It was a form of self expression, and in its way a creative effort. If those who are conscious, however dimly, of an inner lack of fulfilment of their creative instincts could be spurred to find some outlet which demands both mental and physical effort, and go all out to exploit it, any boredom or discontent would vanish.

JAN 74